THE PROCESS OF DYING AND OUR JOURNEY BEYOND

THE PROCESS OF DYING AND OUR JOURNEY BEYOND

What really happens when we shed our physical body!

Dieter G. Gedeik

Dedicated to
my teacher and friend
Dr. Douglas M. Baker, MD

TABLE OF CONTENTS:

ACKNOWLEDGMENTS

Cover artwork by Markus H. Hayward
A fellow truth seeker

FOREWORD

For two thousand years the Westerner has relied solely upon his faith in Christian teachings that man survives beyond the grave. For many of us the words "Faith" and "Believe" are no longer good enough. They imply "not knowing" whereas younger people, born into the new age of Aquarius demand to know and to experience. The search for the purpose of life and the very important subject of life after death has been with me since the age of nine. Much research was done and plenty of personal experience recalled to make this little book possible. May this information encourage you to research further and to bring desperately needed Light and Love to this planet.

Become a knower via studying what the "Ancient Wisdom" teaches us, and let the test of truth be gained via its application to your life. I am sending these words out into the world with no special claim. They are not "inspired" by a higher source and must stand or fall on their own merits. Listen, listen to that yet small voice within.

Ask yourself ... do you want Truth
or just an outer sound of harmony?

The Wisdom is not a religion, philosophy, or science. However, this knowledge can be applied to all of these areas to clarify and enhance your understanding of them. The Wisdom is an independent field of study, experience, and practice. It is to facilitate step-by-step unfoldment from individuality to group awareness, from unconscious activity to conscious cooperation with your Higher Self and Its purpose for you, the personality.

Wisdom concerns the one Self, knowledge deals with the not-self.

Dieter G. Gedeik

CHAPTER I – THE JOURNEY BEGINS

Introduction

Why should you care?

What would you do if your manager at work tells you that she is sending you to a foreign country next month to open a new branch? Would you immediately start preparing for this? Would you quickly check on?

> Visa and inoculation requirements,
> transportation, currency, prices,
> local & labor laws, housing, etc.

Of course, you would!

Whether you shed your physical body tomorrow or in 60 years, you will go to a place you might, right now, know little about!

What you learn and apply right here while in the physical body, will directly determine the quality and duration of your experience as you, the personality in the "Afterlife" - the Astral Plane, Mental Plane and even more illustrious planes! The willful progress you make here can tremendously benefit you, starting even right now.

Are you ready to enter upon this journey of discovering what and who you really are?

"The readiness to initiate the journey cannot be forced
nor can people be faulted if it has not occurred in them as yet.
The level of consciousness has to have advanced to the stage
where such an intention would be meaningful and attractive."

David R. Hawkins

Just as with my previous video series "Introduction to the Ancient Wisdom", most of this information came about while focusing on one word or concept at a time and by comparing the digitized "Classics" written by H. P. Blavatsky, C. W. Leadbeater, Annie Besant, Alice

Bailey, L. Cedercrans, my teacher Douglas M. Baker and many more. Then, I tried to come up with the best way to re-conciliate this information with my personal experiences and present it here for you. I apologize to those teachers if I erred in any way.

For those of you with no esoteric background, I left many, many details out and I encourage you to study the books referenced. Because I present this information in English and in the Western Hemisphere, I will use as many "Christian" words as possible to make this more understandable. I personally do not belong to any religion, sect or cult.

First: I must point out my three-part video "Introduction to the Ancient Wisdom" in order to aid you in understanding better the subject at hand. If you have not seen them yet, go to https://www.douglasbaker.org and click on "The Ancient Wisdom Videos." Parts I through III will prepare you for this writing. They are free to watch as are all of about 74 videos created by my teacher and friend, Dr. Douglas M. Baker, MD. There you will also find about five hundred of his audio lectures and links to his eBooks and printed books. Many of those are translated into eight major European languages and distributed world-wide via Google, Amazon, iTunes Stores, Barnes & Noble and many more.

Second: whenever the words "Death or dying" are used, you can substitute these by "Passing on" or "Focus of self-consciousness to a higher Plane."

There is no death, only change!

Third: I am trying to address the experience of the average person today in the West. At times I will cover certain groups of people and how their experience differs from the norm. You can find a list of references used in the back of this book or download a list of references used from my website https://www.douglasbaker.org, just search for part number 6061.

With this book I shall attempt to answer:

- ❖ What is the purpose of survival?

- ❖ How do we survive the grave?

- ❖ What do we survive in?

- ❖ What sort of environment surrounds us when we survive?

- ❖ Reincarnation, the cycle.

Reality is stranger than the human mind can imagine

Review of the Oneness of Consciousness

In all of my previous writings and videos I tried to instill in the student the idea that all consciousness in this universe is one. To most of you in the West this is a bewildering idea, conjuring up in your mind the loss of self-identity. Much of this concern is amplified by misinterpreted Eastern sayings like *"I am the raindrop, make me the sea"*.

Nothing can be further from the truth! On every level, self-consciousness from the human kingdom on up to the Great Being Who expresses Itself via this universe, is preserved. It is only due to our very limited senses and consciousness that most of us can't comprehend anything else above our physical existence. However, as self-consciousness is raised past the human condition to higher and higher states, it becomes more inclusive and aware of all life forms there on that plane AND below that plane.

> *"Consciousness serves as the vehicle by which Spirit can become self-conscious on all planes of vibration between lowest matter and its source, Spirit."*

Alice A. Bailey

Do you have any idea about "The One in Whom we live and move and have our being"? Man's place in this great scheme of life is not a trivial one. The spiritual part of Man (Monad*) plays a vital role for many eons as the overshadowing and guiding power in the evolution of all kingdoms below ours on this planet. We are the link between the microcosm and the macrocosm.

> *"He who knows others is clever;*
> *He who knows himself has discernment."*

Lao-Tzu

*Monad: The Spark Divine, our pure Spirit.
See my video *"Journey into Consciousness"*

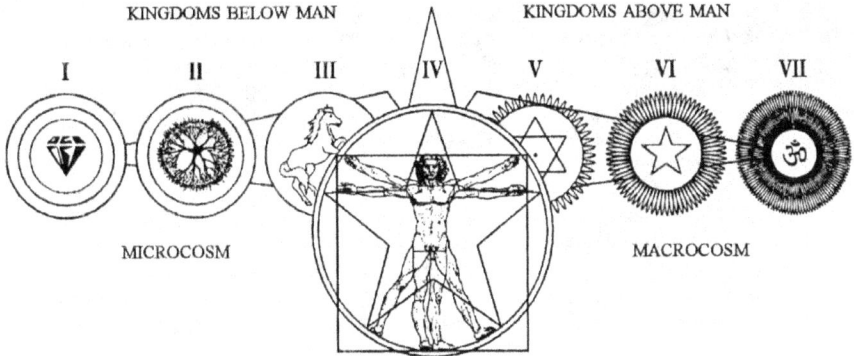

Man as a Balance
WHAT THE KINGDOMS ABOVE ARE TO US;
WE ARE TO THE KINGDOMS BELOW US.
CONTEMPLATE YOUR RESPONSIBILITY!

As Albert Einstein showed us via $E=MC^2$, there is no "solid matter." All is energy, and many of us know that energy follows thought! Most religions have some form of organized prayer groups. The Catholic Church, amongst other types of prayer has prayers of "Supplication/ Petition/Intercession."

Focused and directed thought by individuals or in groups, has been proven capable of transmitting thought - mental energy, world-wide for millennia.

Note to image on the next page: The next page shows a slide from my video *"Journey into Consciousness."* Study the statements on that image well and remember, that your individualized consciousness within that One Great Consciousness is like a tiny concentration within that vast ocean of consciousness which reaches from grossest matter to highest Spirit!

On the left edge I show the Cosmic planes 1-7. Presently, all human evolution takes place within the 7th, physical, or lowest Cosmic plane which is again divided into 7 Cosmic sub-planes.

Here in this book, we are only touching upon the three lowest planes within the Cosmic physical plane: the physical, the astral/emotional and the mental plane.

What is Consciousness? +

SPIRIT/LIFE
Spirit is Matter at its highest vibration

1. Consciousness is the result of the continuous attraction and repulsion between Spirit and Matter.

All Spirit is conditioned by matter!
All consciousness has form!

Consciousness is the medium by which Spirit gains experience in matter.

Consciousness is the evolution of Being or Identity.

Matter is the evolution of intelligence or substance.

CONSCIOUSNESS

2. Consciousness is an electro-magnetic phenomenon vibrating at every frequency between Spirit and Matter!

3. These frequencies are divided into 7 major groups or COSMIC PLANES!

Even the smallest particle of matter is informed by Spirit!

Every form is conscious!

MATTER/FOR
Matter is Spirit at its lowest vibration

Cosmic Physical Plane

7 Planes of our Solar System

THIS IS THE AREA OF CONSCIOUSNESS THIS BOOK IS DEALING WITH!
THE PHYSICAL, THE ASTRAL/EMOTIONAL AND THE MENTAL
PLANE. (First three sub-planes of the Cosmic-physical plane)

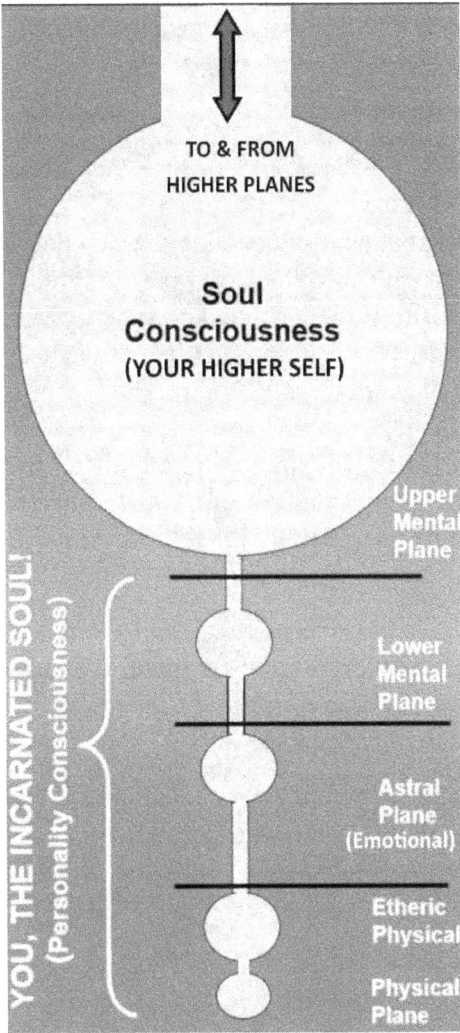

To & From Higher Planes

Soul Consciousness
(YOUR HIGHER SELF)

Upper Mental Plane

Lower Mental Plane

Astral Plane (Emotional)

Etheric Physical

Physical Plane

YOU, THE INCARNATED SOUL! (Personality Consciousness)

With this very brief review of consciousness between the physical plane, the mental plane and beyond, I attempt to show that: **ALL CONSCIOUSNESS IS ONE!**

Image at left: The personality has attracted matter of that particular plane it is functioning on. Here it is shown pulled apart but in reality, all matter, planes and consciousness exist in the same space and time. Like sand intermingles with water and water with gas in solution. Each made up of smaller bits.

It is only via false teachings, development of the Soul and lack of training, that Man presently is only self-conscious in his physical brain!

Incarnation starts when we establish first the mental body, then the astral (emotional) body and finally the etheric and physical body.

These vehicles and concentrations of Soul-consciousness we refer to as "THE INCARNATED SOUL" and the accumulation of physical, emotional and mental energy make up the personality, guided to whatever extent possible by the Soul.

It is said, ... *as you earnestly take charge of your own evolution, your consciousness doubles every year!*

What We Really Are

Now we should contemplate what and who we really are and come to the realization that we are so much more than we were taught. If what I now tell you causes conflict in you... good. The journey you are taking is that of self-identification. Every step on this path causes you to identify yourself as part of something greater. This in turn initially causes doubt and confusion. In my free video *"I the Personality, ... I the Soul, ... I the Monad"* I explain in more detail the trials and tribulations we have to go through as our consciousness expands and we seek self-identification. Stick with it, and you will succeed.

We are not our physical body, nor our emotions, not even our thoughts. We must recognize them as energies and attributes we have appropriated and put to use for the purpose of building a personality so that we can function within these lower planes.

In our true nature we are not men or women, male or female. We are not a king, queen, husband, wife, shoe salesperson, business executive, etc. We acquired these attributes since birth to survive, communicate and succeed.

Conventional psychology tells us we are product of two determinants:

1. **GENETICS,** hereditary equipment (Via DNA).

2. **ENVIRONMENTAL FACTORS** like schooling, peer ship influence, parenting.

BUT; The Ancient Wisdom states that the most important aspect which creates, nourishes and overshadows the personality is the Soul.

3. THE SOUL, OUR HIGHER SELF, becoming more and more self-conscious on planes below It via the personality and the three lower vehicles It created. It is the "maturity" of the Soul and to what extent it can reflect Soul qualities via its personality here on Earth that makes us so different. The Soul is an entity which is evolving by experiences. It is not a spirit, but it is a vehicle of spirit - the Monad.

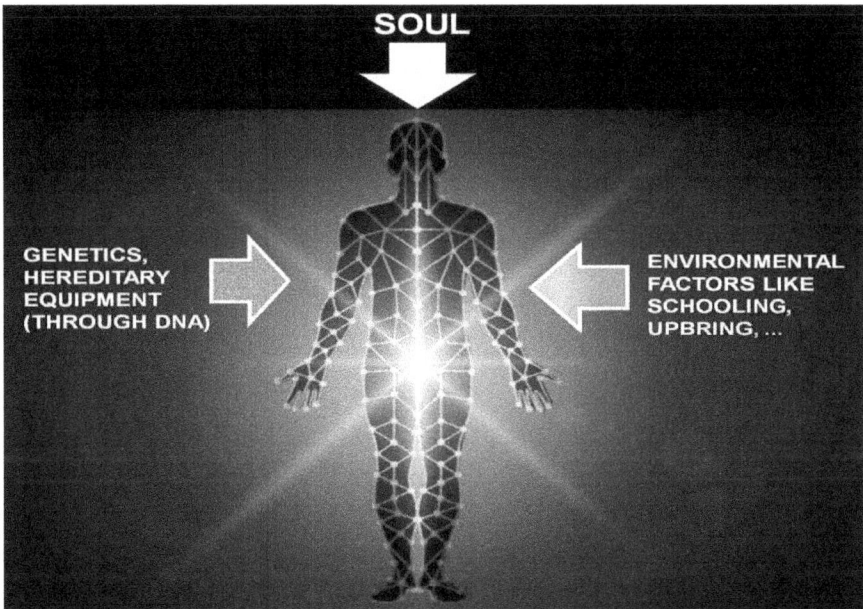

This third factor includes the essence within us, different from human to human and yet a common source within all of us. It incorporates all those obscure or hidden factors untraceable to our heredity equipment or environment but which seem to hold us together, imbue us with life and make us spiritually creative. We call it the "Soul", "Higher Self", "Higher Consciousness", "Solar Angel" and know it by many other names. This is also the part that brings in our ancient and more recent karma.

The common belief that Christianity was first to teach the existence of the Soul is simply wrong. Six hundred years before, Socrates and Plato in ancient Greece talked about the human Soul and the many reincarnations It must experience before reaching "Perfection." And even eons before that, the ancient teachings in India were well aware of our higher consciousness, the atman, the Soul.

THREE GREAT TRUTHS

Hear me, my brother, he said. "There are three truths which are absolute, and which cannot be lost, but yet may remain silent for lack of speech."

The soul of man is immortal, and its future is the future of a thing whose growth and splendour has no limit.

The principle which gives life dwells in us and without us, is undying and eternally beneficent, is-not heard or seen, or smelt, but is perceived by the man who desires perception.

Each man is his own absolute lawgiver, the dispenser of glory or gloom to himself; the decreer of his life, his reward, his punishment;

These truths, which are as great as is life itself, are as simple as the simplest mind of man. Feed the hungry with them.

The Idyll of The White Lotus
Mabel Collins

We are so much more than is apparent to our five senses. **We are truly Spirit having a human experience!** I tell you this not to booster your belief of self-importance, for that is truly the most difficult illusion to overcome. It is with humility and malleability that we must approach any new subject in order to learn. It would be an irrational proposition to learn a new paradigm without change in your thinking.

For the mind to flower it has to go beyond what it knows."

Mother Meera

We are the incarnated Soul, having "externalized" vehicles of consciousness like the physical, emotional and mental bodies. In so doing, we limited or "buried" our true nature and powers to the point where today many people believe they are no more than a physical, emotional and mental being. Some even believe that they are just the outcome of chemical reactions and biological processes.

The personality that came about isolated itself via false teachings and the need to survive, and our true Self, the Soul, lost virtually all influence as the person grew up and the personality matured. This is often referred to as the "death" of the Soul. Because we imprisoned ourselves in form or substance, our next "death" is the process of release from that form. We must realize that the final objective is the complete liberation of all consciousness from form on the physical, astral/emotional and lower mental planes and the harvesting of all that is good into our higher Self, the Soul.

Only equipped with this knowledge will you understand the process of "Death and Beyond!"

"Our birth is but a sleep and a forgetting;

The soul that rises with us, our life's star,

Hath had elsewhere its setting

And cometh from afar;

Not in entire forgetfulness,

And not in utter nakedness,

But trailing clouds of glory do we come

From God who is our home:

Heaven lies about us in our infancy!

Shades of the prison-house begin to close

Upon the growing Boy,

But he beholds the light, and whence it flows,

He sees it in his joy.

The youth, who daily farther from the East

Must travel, still is Nature's priest,

And by the vision splendid

Is on his way attended;

At length the Man perceives it die away,

And fade into the light of common day. "

Wordsworth's *"Ode on Intimations of Immortality"*
from *"Recollections of Early Childhood."*

Why are we here, and what is the purpose of our life?

In my video "I the Personality, … I the Soul, … I the Monad" I explain in more detail our purpose here and now:

❖ It is the evolution of consciousness and becoming self-conscious on all planes.

❖ To manifest the highest and most spiritual qualities and deeds as personality. This is how we, the Soul, grow.

❖ To aid our fellow brothers and sisters and attune ourselves to the purpose of this incarnation.

❖ To become conscious of our part in this grand scheme of life and aid in the evolution of humanity and this planet.

❖ Death, birth and karma are all part of the cycle of reincarnation and must be considered together. Death is the recall of all good experiences into the Soul.

The early Christian church taught reincarnation but removed it from the scriptures about 553 AD. Then, for obvious reasons, the church made itself the gate keeper to heaven and the forgiver of sins. None the less, the theme of reincarnation continues in Christianity despite of this. Even today, 25% of Christians (2015 survey) believe in reincarnation.

The lack of right knowledge and false teachings about what comes after physical death created the prevailing fear about this process. The great un-known stains all anticipation as negative and frightening.

LET'S CHANGE THAT! There is no death,
only change of state and entrance into a fuller life.

Today, the majority of people on the planet believe that we are reborn again and again. They also believe that when all human karma is resolved and our true nature is "perfected," rebirth into human life is done and we move into the next higher kingdom.

I died a mineral, and became a plant.
I died a plant and rose an animal.
I died an animal and I was man.
Why should I fear?
When was I less by dying?
Yet once more, I shall die as Man,
to soar with angels blest;
But even from angelhood,
I must pass on.

Jalal – Uddin, Rumi

CHAPTER II – PHYSICAL DEATH

General Statements

"There is a technique of dying just as there is of living".

A Treatise on White Magic,
Alice A. Bailey.

"Our Ideas about death have been erroneous; we have looked upon it as the great and ultimate terror, whereas in reality it is the great escape, the entrance into a fuller measure of activity, and the release of the life from the crystallised vehicle and an inadequate form."

The Consciousness of the Atom
Alice A. Bailey.

This portion of the journey, starting with the shedding of the physical body is part of the cycle we call REINCARNATION. In this writing, I will only outline what the Ancient Wisdom refers to as "Restitution, Elimination and Integration". It covers physical death up to the final "Transfer of focus for the distribution of energy from the personality … to the Soul."

It is my sincere hope that one day in the minds of those left behind, sorrow will find no place and the deathbed will be regarded as a happy occasion like births and marriages. Right knowledge is the key to bring this about!

AWAKE … AWAKE, … AWAKE TO DREAMS NO MORE

A Great Teacher

Nightly sleep can be considered as occasional dying! The only difference between sleep and death is that in sleep the magnetic thread or current of energy (Sutratma) along which the life force streams (between Soul and sinus node of the heart) is preserved intact.

The so-called "silver cord" still connecting us is actually a stream of energy from a much higher source.

This stream of life force is the path of return to the physical body. Once severed, physical death ensues.

During sleep, we spend much of our time withdrawn from the physical-etheric bodies, and when we are fully aware of this fact, we call it an out-of-body experience. In the sleep state, we use the astral body as a vehicle for our consciousness. Control of this body by a fully alert mind represents astral projection.

When sleeping, we are far more able to assimilate prana than while we are awake, and the atmosphere has more prana in the first hours of the night than later. This recharging is made possible when the etheric body slips slightly out of alignment with the physical body.

There are many ways we know death can happen and each type of person will experience a different transition. One of these can be that the Soul desires to initiate physical death in order to more rapidly obliterate past karma, or terminate an incarnation if the personality strays too far from its "Fixed Design," its purpose. Another reason could be that the purpose for this incarnation was fulfilled and no more could be gained.

Here we will explore just a few. And again, for easier reading many details were left out. Please study the materials pointed out in the list of references, part #6061 at https://www.douglasbaker.org.

We will look at:

❖ **The average good person, elderly or mature adult dying of a disease.**

❖ **Sudden accidental and war-death.**

❖ **Suicides and consequences.**

❖ **Young children and babies.**

❖ **Unevolved People**

❖ **Earth-bound good and bad people.**

❖ **Aspirants, accepted disciples and initiates.**

So called evil humans and lost souls we will deal with in the section "Introduction to "Hell.""

As I have explained in my videos, almost all persons are presently only self-conscious in the physical brain. Self-consciousness is that which allows you to recognize yourself, apart from the group as an individual. All life forms are conscious but not necessarily self-conscious!

Further, an average person's self-consciousness always resides in the outer-most body (physical brain). So, when you shed your physical body, your self-consciousness (YOU, the "I" the "THINKER") has no choice but to transfer into the next densest vehicle which is your astral body.

Shedding the Physical Body

Restitution

Esoteric term for willingly and gladly rendering or giving back the substance of the physical body to its source and of restoring the Soul to its essential being. Death will become a normal and understood process one day.

The Average Good Person, Elderly or Mature Adult Dying of a Disease

When the person has a terminal illness and there is little hope of a recovery, it is most certain that it is the Soul recalling its personal self (the personality).

When it has been determined that the death of the person is imminent, silence should be maintained and only orange light be used. This will help the Soul to hold possession with clarity until the last minute.

90% of the time when a dying person is in what appears to be a coma, they are fully conscious! No music, mantras or singing is recommended. If possible, the top of the head should be pointed to the East, feet and hands crossed. If incense is used, then only Sandalwood. Here I recommend only what is safe for the general public to know at this time.

The Ancient Wisdom tells us: (much of what follows you will find in *Esoteric Healing, A Treatise on the Seven Rays, vol IV, The Act of Restitution,* pages 460-478. By Alice A. Bailey)

❖ The Soul sounds forth a word of withdrawal and the physical body responds immediately.

❖ Physiological changes take place at the seat of the disease, then in the blood stream, the nervous system and the endocrine system.

- ❖ A vibration runs along the Nadis (the etheric counterpart of the entire nervous system). The Nadis react to the "pull" of the Soul and organize themselves for abstraction.

- ❖ The bloodstream becomes affected in a peculiar occult manner. This is caused by the glandular system injecting a substance into the blood which in turn effects the heart. That's where the life-thread is anchored and this substance is one of the causes of coma and loss of consciousness. It evokes a reflex action in the brain.

- ❖ A psychic tremor is established, loosening or breaking the connections between the Nadis and the nervous system. The etheric body is thereby detached from the dense physical body but still interpenetrates it. The Sutratma life strand anchored in the sinus node of the heart is withdrawn.

- ❖ A pause frequently ensues to carry forward the loosening process and to allow this to be as smooth and painless as possible. This process starts in the eyes. It promotes relaxation, lack of fear, peace, willingness to let go and the inability to mentally fight the process. The dying person's consciousness is still preserved.

- ❖ The etheric body begins to gather itself at the point of exit, loosened from the nervous system. It begins to withdraw first from the extremities via one of the "exits." For the average emotional person this is the Solar Plexus. For the more spiritual, kindly person and some aspirants it is the area just below the apex of the heart.

For the intellectual, spiritually advanced person, disciples and initiates the exit is the area of the Bregma, also called in babies the anterior fontanelle at the top of the head. Exit here assures continuity of consciousness during the transition. See next image.

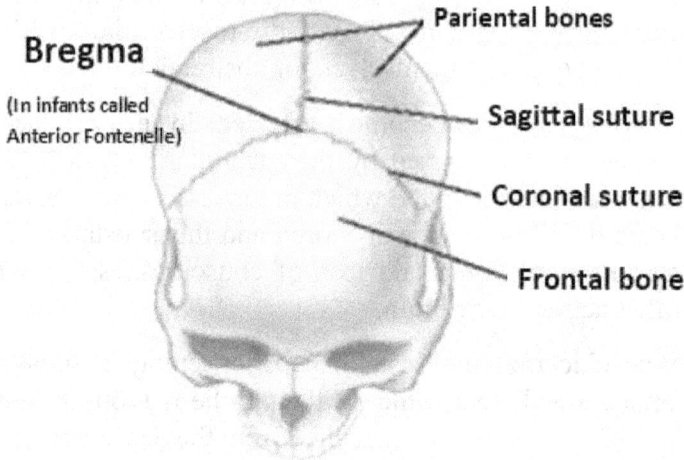

Bregma

(In infants called
Anterior Fontenelle)

Pariental bones

Sagittal suture

Coronal suture

Frontal bone

❖ As the final withdrawal of the person's consciousness proceeds, the vague, instinctual consciousness of the physical body's "Elemental of Appearance" (some call it Deva of Appearance) begins to resist the pull of the Soul. As explained in my previous videos, this physical elemental is in total the "Spirit of the earth" and is on the involutionary arc and opposes the Soul's work to raise man towards Spirit. It is the Elemental's instinct to preserve its physical form and it fights dissolution.

❖ But death is not yet complete, for the brain is the last organ of the physical body to die. For some time after the heart has ceased beating, the brain and its memory still remain active and, although unconsciously so, the human ego for this short length of time, passes in review every event of the preceding life.

❖ This great or small panoramic picture of the past (Akashic Records) is purely automatic. The person watches this wonderful review scene by scene, a review which includes the entire course of thought, action and emotions of the life just closed. This review serves to sort out the best and noblest parts and preserve them for the life to come in the mental plane.

Based on my own personal experience, this in duration as measured by us takes only a few seconds to two minutes. Time at this moment seems to not follow the same clock as it does in our physical world.

The scenes run backwards towards childhood and are so brilliantly clear, precise, detailed and in color, that our present-day physical brain memory is a washed-out blur in comparison. All the emotions and memories of those events are re-lived. These scenes, down to the smallest detail are the truth, the real ones, even though we forgot them a long time ago.

When the scenes digress to infancy and birth, the Sutratma's connection in the third ventricle of the physical brain is withdrawn by the Soul. This stream of energy is called the consciousness thread.

❖ Then follows a brilliant flaring-up of pure electric light and the "Body of Light" finally breaks all contact with the dense physical vehicle, focuses for a short period in the vital (etheric) body and then disappears. This radiant inner body of light is present in each individual, unseen and unrevealed, but is slowly becoming stronger with each incarnation. It is an early prelude to the transfiguration experience. The act of restitution is now accomplished.

❖ The etheric body has now emerged from the physical body and has assumed the vague outline of the form that it previously energized. There is still a slight rapport between the two, and this keeps the spiritual man, (the Soul in His astral body & mental vehicle) still close to the body just vacated. This is one of the many reasons cremation of the physical body is so important! It hastens the release of the person from the physical – etheric body in a few hours instead of a few days.

The person's individuality is not lost, it still persists, is still in touch with the qualitative and mental processes of existence, remembering all from his physical life. He now stands in his astral/mental body.

Now, depending on the development of the astral/mental body, some fall asleep while many others consciously move through a "tunnel" towards a bright light at its end.

It seems that the tunnel phenomenon serves as a shield to protect the individual from an awareness of the lower portions of the astral world. It is a shift in consciousness from one level to another. More on this in the chapter "Life in the Astral plane and Elimination".

I am here not writing about the "Near Death" or "Out-of-Body" experiences so well investigated, documented and proven. Thousands of cases were examined and found valid by medical professionals. Many documentaries can be found on Netflix and social platforms. Just keep your guards up and use your critical faculties.

As a final thought I must add this; in today's Western World, too many terminally sick are kept alive beyond their wish and the intent of the Soul. Lack of understanding death, monetary interest and legalities complicate the dying process today.

Too many of us mourn the loss to us, a selfish sentiment. The one departed starts a much more liberated, painless way of life. The uncontrolled, intense grief by a remaining relative can seriously retard the disembodied person's advancement towards the astral and mental world!

Asking the dying to somehow give a sign of life from the astral world is not fair and can almost never be done by the real, departed consciousness. There are natural rules against that and I don't recommend employing a "psychic" to do it for you. This might even cause substantial harm to the one now in the astral plane.

I just turn off when I see a "medium" addressing a large group of people *"I am given the name John, ... does anybody know a John?"* Many "Mental Psychics" gain the information from people's solar plexus area, the emotional center. As closer the real departed individual rises towards the mental plane, as less likely it is that a psychic can create a contact with the departed.

There are of course real, well trained and highly skilled "Psychics" who research and teach, but rarely in public.

Sudden Accidental and War-death

In cases of sudden death through accident, suicide, murder, unexpected heart attacks or through the action of war, the shock is such that the somewhat unhurried process of Soul withdrawal is entirely preempted.

The vacating of the physical body and the complete dissolution of the etheric body occurs in most situations almost simultaneously. The physical elemental has no chance to oppose the vacating of the physical form. The suddenness is felt like an instant and overwhelming sense of imminent peril and destruction and something closely resembling an electric shock.

Some in their desperate struggle to stay in the physical body might draw temporarily some physical materials from the corpse into their etheric body and for a short while reappear visible to normal sight. I observed this once when a car at a very high speed crashed into a power pole outside our house and the driver died on the property.

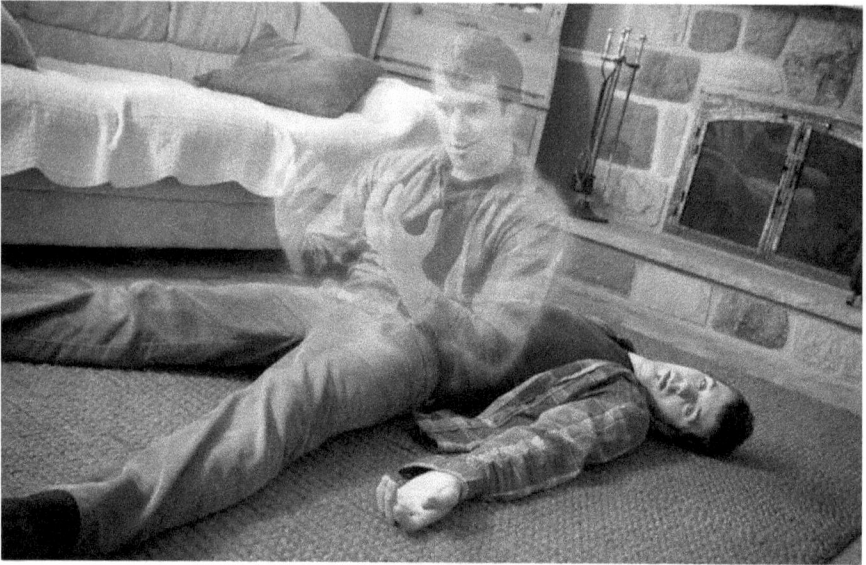

**MOST PEOPLE DO NOT REALIZE THAT
THEY LOST THE PHYSICAL BODY.**

Other than suicide, for sudden death victims, the law of karma is almost never involved and it is not a Soul controlled process. It is not considered an act of restitution.

For the average good person after a few moments to a few hours, life into and in the astral world continues in full consciousness and with the same interests. Like most people they are unaware that they have passed through the episode of physical death.

Such individuals, cut short in life by accident or suicide, must frequently spend a period here as long as their life would have been on Earth under karmic law.

A different path ensues for those of less desirable characters like criminals, materialistically oriented, etc... They, for various lengths of time must remain close to the earth near their old environment in a state we call "earth-bound." They seek desperately and by every possible means to contact it and to re-enter their old life.

In all cases there has been no destruction of human self-identity!

Suicides and Consequences

This is mostly a violation of the Soul's plan or "Fixed Design" and negative karma is created that might take several life-times to be worked out. Under karmic law, suicides must frequently spend in the astral world a period as long as their natural life would have been in the physical body.

Depending on the circumstances and other factors, many suicide victims must forgo the "heaven world" (mental plane) and reincarnate soon after life on the astral plane. In the astral (emotional) plane that which they tried to escape from will hound them but is substantially amplified. Remember, this is the emotional, feeling and desire plane.

INSTEAD OF HAVING ESCAPED THEIR PROBLEM, THEY NOW SUFFER EVEN MORE INTENSELY.

Suicides undergo the same separation from their physical body as an accidental or sudden death victim. Suicide for a very noble cause is rare and their experience and karmic consequences can differ substantially.

Assisted suicide is another questionable subject and can substantially work against the will of the Soul. Who are we to know the karma of such person and to what extent the otherwise remaining suffering was meant to burn off additional karma?

That is why I removed all firearms from the house of a family member dying of cancer. This, and much information given about the life hereafter prevented a likely suicide and made his transition easier.

Suicides are steadily on the rise as we develop and refine our physical and astral (feeling) bodies. In those areas, this made us substantially more sensitive to stress and pain. It has also become fairly clear that the advent of cell phones, tablets, personal computers and the Internet have tremendously increased young people's exposure to much good and bad information. Unfortunately, negative information is gaining more focus and re-distribution.

Other factors are overpopulation and ever-increasing difficulties and stresses of modern life. Many younger persons, bewildered by the complexities of the world they live in, want answers which today's schooling, most parents and religions cannot provide. **They are not taught how they fit into the greater scheme of our complex existence.** Thy look for a <u>purpose</u> for their mental and emotional suffering, and can't find one! The children and teenagers become overwhelmed, confused, depressed and try to find a way out.

It is my hope that books like this one will contribute to the process of psychological integration and lessen the growing tendency towards suicide by providing a wider, richer vision of the purpose of life. Another great stride towards elimination of suicides would be knowing about, striving for, and reaching Soul contact. Then my friends, you will never walk alone again! I describe this contact in my video *"I the Personality, ... I the Soul, ... I the Monad."*

Here is something for your contemplation: As I write this, the Covid-19 pandemic is in full swing and the vast majority of all infected people in the USA entering hospital care, refused to be vaccinated. Those unvaccinated have a 11.3 times higher chance of dying from the virus! Further, the consequences are pain and horrendous stress on family members, care givers and facilities.

Is this situation some form of suicide? What kind of karma is created, or is it the will of their Soul if they die? Man was given free will how to live, but not necessarily about how to die.

Last but not least, I must mention another negative aspect of suicides. Suicides, in rare cases, anxious to undo the deed, try to get in contact with earth again. In their panic and desperation, they might succeed in possessing those incarnate people who are physically feeble and intellectually weak. An act with very serious consequences.

Young Children and Babies

The Soul takes "possession" of the body when the infant is ready to enter the world. This is what brings on the process of labor and birth. This moment was proceeded nine months before by the Soul's creation of a right space in time for conception to take place to further Its plan for that incarnation.

Prior to the seventh year, the strength and vitality of the physical-etheric body is largely the determining factor at death. The etheric, astral and mental vehicles are many times no more than a sheath. The Soul's focus is in the etheric body and It applies just a gently pulsating control and activity. This is sufficient to preserve consciousness, to vitalize the various physical processes, and to begin to form the character and personality. Remember that it is the Soul that vitalizes the physical body via the etheric body.

When a baby's physical death occurs due to an illness or accident, his or her astral nature may be quickly absorbed into the astral body of the mother or sometimes even the father. The reason for this is that most of the child's astral and mental matter was initially "drawn" from the parents, especially from the mother.

The fact that during the very early years the mother and the father donated their astral matter to the child is very important. It created a lasting, hopefully balanced bond between them. But, many behavioral problems in the child's relationship to the mother or father later in life can be traced back to an unequal, unbalanced contribution to the infant's astral (emotional) body. Contemplate the importance of this!

Sample: If a male infant only or mostly receives its astral (emotional) matter from the mother, it might become a <u>contributing</u> factor later for the child to express homosexual karma.

But if the astral body of a child is sufficiently integrated, they will go on into the astral world and grow up for the duration of the Soul's intent. In all cases the consciousness's exit would be via the solar plexus area, about two inches above the belly button. The physical elemental puts up resistance, but restitution is quick.

For those infants and children with insufficiently formed astral bodies, another incarnation attempt by the Soul follows quickly.

Here is what C. W. Leadbeater stated:

> *"Babies not having built a sufficient astral and mental body are not responsible for their actions and cannot receive either reward or punishment. They begin a new life (incarnation) immediately."*

Unevolved People

For the unevolved, physical death is a gentle falling asleep and dreaming about the life just past. The mind in this case is not sufficiently developed. The mental body is a mere outline. This group of people is rapidly shrinking with the fast mental development taking place today.

More on this in the chapter "Life in the Astral Plane."

Earth-bound Good and Bad People

These might be good people who lost their physical body while worrying about loved ones like children and spouses suddenly left behind. Some of those parents are drawn so strongly by love and concern to their children, that they for some years hover near them to observe and guide them.

MOTHER HELD BACK FROM MOVING ON

Here, you also find the cruel, selfish and criminal minded and those primarily interested in materialistic pursuit.

Others who become earth-bound might be those who are highly concerned over their business affairs. Some might want to undo an evil act they committed to clear their conscience. These people go through the normal process described earlier but might fight the process of dying along with the physical elemental, making the transition so much more difficult. More about this in the chapter "Life in the Astral & Elimination."

Some of those earth-bound "bad" people are the extremely materialistically oriented, the severe drug addicts and the alcoholics. I mentioned these previously under "Sudden Accidental and War-death."

These will also fight physical death and their vices will draw them as close as possible to the lower planes of the astral.

Aspirants, Disciples and Initiates

First, I need to explain these titles.

An aspirant is a student aspiring, who is eager and strongly motivated by an "inner" voice to take up serious study and to enter upon the path of enforced, personal spiritual advance. He is also called a probationary disciple.

A disciple has entered the "Path" and is in his Master's ashram, being trained and quickly working towards his first initiation. The word "Disciple" here has nothing to do with religion.

Initiates as the word suggests have received the first, second or third initiation. These are first and foremost determined by their evolving consciousness and skill to do work under the direction of their Teacher and Soul. Much more on this in my video *"I the Personality, ... I the Soul, ... I the Monad."*

With disciples and aspirants, while leaving the physical body, the conflict is more mental and is often focused on the will-to-serve, to fulfill a particular aspect of the Plan for humanity and to return in full consciousness to that work. It is for them an entrance into a familiar world they until now only spent nightly a few hours in. They now can function "around the clock" in their field of service. In the initiates mind there is no conflict, only a conscious and deliberate withdrawal.

The third initiation results in the complete liberation from the "pull" of physical, astral and mental substance so that restitution and elimination is a very quick and controlled process. If there is a slight conflict, it will be between the physical elemental and the mental life remaining in the personality. In all three above, the disintegration of the etheric body can be very rapid. The exit occurs in full consciousness via the head region within the area of the Bregma. This site is the only point by which conscious exit is accomplished. Exiting via the solar plexus and heart area causes the person to make the transition mostly in a sleep-state.

The Case for Cremation

"CREMATION IS KINDER TO THE DEAD, better for Humanity itself, and will become of even greater concern to environmentalists anxious to purify the planet and to prevent its further pollution."

"What could be worse than polluting the soil of the Earth with disease-ridden bodies discarded at death which could so easily be vaulted out of their resting places by any geophysical cataclysm to pollute the Earth once more?

It should never be forgotten that those virus conditions which often cause death, like the influenza virus of 1918, are crystalline in structure and can survive in dead bodies in the soil indefinitely and have been responsible for several world epidemics."

Life after Death,
by Dr. Douglas M. Baker

How true, especially as we are right now in the midst of a Covid-19 pandemic, wondering where this virus came from. All a virus in its crystallized form needs is warmth and liquid, found so readily in the air-passages of animals or humans.

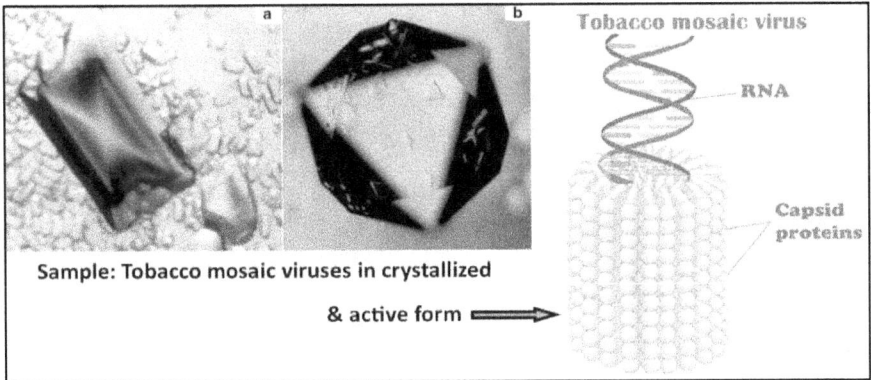

Sample: Tobacco mosaic viruses in crystallized

& active form ➡

Organ Donations

Those of you who consider this should know, that to a certain extent, you will share the karma with the recipient and vice-versa! This could influence your duration and quality of astral and mental plane life. It creates a very subtle bond between the donor and the recipient as long as the donated part has the original matter within it. I advise against it.

Now that science harvests or creates certain parts and organs for human implantations using specially bred animals, I encourage the reader to research the subject in the esoteric classical literature. It is a subject requiring very serious consideration. A person of low character would definitely be influenced negatively.

Giving blood is much more benign. Red blood cells tend to live only about 120 days. 1% of whole blood is made up by white blood cells (leucocytes) but they live from just hours to years. Platelet's lifespan is 9-12 days. Use of the plasma only should be fine.

The Etheric Body

Also called the etheric double and vitality body. Occultly, as long as the etheric shell exists, it is faintly linked to the departed Soul and personality. The etheric body is still part of our physical makeup, consisting of ions, protons, neutrinos and electrons. This burdens the continuing process of the life in the astral world. Cremation hastens this separation and prevents negative or elemental forces to use this etheric shell for their purpose (like Poltergeists). Cremation also helps to purify the astral plane by reducing the aspect of desire to cling to physical life.

The preservation of the body like mummification substantially increases the time the personality has to spend in the astral world before moving into higher planes. This could be hundreds of years of resisting the Soul's attracting love to carry forwards the process of dying!

> *"..... (There remains) on the other side of the threshold of physical life, (in) the etheric world — the "shadow" of the man that was. The ancients called these human shadows, shades; modern children and nursemaids call them ghosts and spooks; and each such shade is but an eidolon, or astral image or pale copy of the physical man that was.*

> *This eidolon coheres for a while in the astral realms or in the super-physical ether (etheric), and its particles are magnetically held more or less coherent as long as the physical corpse is not fully dissolved into its component elements; but these eidola in a comparatively short time fade out, for they decay in a manner closely resembling the disintegration of the physical body."*

> Occult Glossary, by G. de Purucker
> (in brackets added by the author)

Chapter Summary

❖ Dying has many important functions, without which immortality* would not be possible. In death, we discard the worn-out remains of our physical vehicle, corrupted as they are by disease, aging, injury and sheer abuse.

* Here the term "immortality" supposes timelessness and teaches that this timelessness exists for that which is not perishable or conditioned by time. This term is only meaningful while we have a physical brain.

❖ There is no angry, vengeful God, no hell and eternal damnation as we are told and no terrible punishment via Him. While here in the physical (incarnation), the Soul and its personality constantly perform actions, causing reactions; ... CAUSE and EFFECT. The consequences of these actions we call good or bad karma. It is actually right here, in physical existence, in which we must atone and work out our karma. It is here in this plane in which suffering of every sort of pain takes place for almost all of us. However, there are exceptions.

❖ Those of us on the "Path of enforced evolution" find our karma sped up, consequences amplified, and at times we are given additional challenges to work off group and planetary karma. Most of the karma all of humanity is collectively working off is that of "The One in Whom we live and move and have our being." Remember, presently this is the only planet in the Solar System where physical pain can be experienced. The law of karma applies to everyone above the animal kingdom!

❖ Restitution results in the dissolution of the physical body and the return of its elements, atoms and cells to their originating source.

❖ The moment immediately preceding death from disease is that of total insensitivity to pain. Instead, we experience a delightful passivity. Restitution should be a happy occasion and is as important as birth. However, this must never encourage suicide!

❖ Cremation of the physical body must prevail over burial from now on. Longing for the physical earth-life will also prolong the escape from the astral plane. Many future pandemics can be avoided this way.

❖ You have to weigh the positive and negative karmic consequences of organ and blood donations. Blood donations are much more benign since those cells normally live a much shorter time. Using animal derived parts or cells within the human body can have a whole new group of consequences.

There is a flame within me that has stood

Unmoved, untroubled through a mist of years,

Knowing not love nor laughter, hope nor fears,

Nor foolish throb of ill, nor wine of good.

I feel no shadow of the winds that brood,

I hear no whisper of a tide that veers,

I weave no thought of passion, nor of tears,

Unfettered I of time, of habitude.

I know no birth; I know no death that chills;

I fear no fate nor fashion, cause nor creed,

I shall outdream the slumber of the hills,

I am the bud, the flower, I the seed:

For I do know that in whate'er I see

I am the part and it the soul of me.

Quiet
by John Spencer Muirhead

Chapter III – "HELL"

Introduction to "Hell"

Here we briefly touch upon the so-called "Hell." There is a real location and state of consciousness so depraved and evil, that redemption in the astral is almost impossible. There are even today such groups of people on this planet who willingly and on purpose become Soul-less.

Their desire is to become as influential and wealthy by any means and remain in the physical as long as possible. It is total misuse of energies for selfish purposes and is known as the "black arts." Some of those even call themselves a "religion."

There is an appropriate sphere for every degree of development of the human condition. Each is magnetically attracted to that appropriate sphere of vibrational matter and consciousness and remains there until it is thoroughly purged of their condition or the Soul is destroyed; a very rare occurrence on this planet.

Avitchi & and the Eighth Sphere or Planet of Death

There is a state that comes close to what could be called "Hell." Let us see what the teachers of the Ancient Wisdom tell us about the subject:

> *"The teaching is, simply, that each entity after physical death is drawn to the appropriate sphere to which the karmic destiny of entity and the entity's own character and impulses magnetically attract it. As a man works, as a man sows, in his life, that and that only shall he reap after death."*

> *"... Avîchi* has many degrees or grades. Nature has all things in her; if she has heavens where good and true men find rest and peace and bliss, so has she other spheres and states where gravitate those who must find an outlet for the evil passions burning within.*

> *They, at the end of their avîchi, go to pieces and are ground over and over, and vanish away finally like a shadow before the sunlight in the air — ground over in nature's laboratory."*

Occult Glossary, G. de Purucker
* Sanskrit spelling

"The Eighth Sphere" ... "Frequently the term is confused with avîchi (q.v.), but this is incorrect, because the two, while closely connected, are nevertheless quite distinct. While avîchi is a state where very evil human beings "die and are reborn without interruption," yet not without hope of final redemption — something which can actually take place even on our physical plane in the cases of very evil or soulless men — the Eighth Sphere represents a degree of psycho-mental degeneration still more advanced.

As just hinted, even in avîchi there is a possibility of reinsoulment by the ray of the spiritual Monad; whereas in the Eighth Sphere or Planet of Death such possibility finally vanishes, and the entity which has sunk to the Planet of Death is what is technically called in the esoteric philosophy a "lost soul." In the Eighth Sphere the lost souls are ground over and over in nature's laboratory, and are finally dissipated into their component psycho-astral elements or life-atoms.

The Eighth Sphere or Planet of Death is an actual globe. It is also of course a state or condition of being; whereas the avîchi is almost exclusively a state or condition in which an entity may find itself, although obviously this entity must have position or place and therefore locality in space — on our earth or elsewhere.

Occult Glossary, G. de Purucker

"Avitchi: A state of consciousness, not necessarily after death or between births for it can take place on earth as well. Literally it means "uninterrupted hell." The last of the eight hells we are told where "the culprits die and are reborn without interruption – yet not without hope of final redemption."

The Secret Doctrine, Vol. III,
p. 510, 521, 528, 529
by H. P. Blavatsky.

.... "Where, however, it is the result of deliberate choice, or of preference for wrong action, in spite of knowledge and in defiance of the voice of the spiritual nature, then this type of karma leads to what the oriental occultist called "avitchi" or the eighth sphere, — a term synonymous with the Christian idea of the condition of being a lost soul. These cases are, however, exceedingly rare, and have relation to the left-hand path, and the practice of black magic.

Though this condition involves the severing of the highest principle (that of pure spirit from its two expressions, the soul and the body, or from the six lower principles), yet the life itself remains, and after the destruction of the soul in avitchi, a fresh cycle of becoming will again be offered." (By the Monad *)

The Light of the Soul, Book IV, page 391,
by Alice A. Bailey
*Added by author.

On one occasion in such realm, I observed a person being exposed to the results of his own actions. In physical life, on several occasions on rail platforms he pushed unsuspecting victims into the path of oncoming trains. Now in avitchi I saw him standing on the rail track being "killed" instantly by a very fast train. He was immediately "reborn" and standing again on the track, facing a rapidly approaching train, only to be hit again.

After the third time observing this horrendous spectacle, I asked my "Companion," "How many times will this be repeated?" The reply came as a surprise to me. "It will take two thousand times" I was told! For a second, I thought I might have perceived wrong. And as I was leaving that place, I debated with myself the pros and cons of such a situation. In this case he will pay for his actions with "like" punishment which is not necessarily the norm.

We know that karmic law weighs positive against negative energy. Hence, a good deed may nullify a bad deed of equal proportion or at least lessen its resolution. Our little minds can't comprehend the actions of the four "Lipika Lords of Karma" and the tabularization of the akashic records yet. In the Christian world they are referred to as the "Recording Angels" and "keeping of the book."

Here is another example of life within this realm from my diary:

"Sept. 15th, 2008.

I was taken to a place where evil dwells. Very powerful, negative vibrations threatened to overcome my defenses.

The word Avitchi or hell came to mind. I found myself in the place where the worst of humanity after physical death gravitate, to find an outlet for their evil appetites.

There was so much evil here, that those "inmates" in charge had established prisons (cages) within this "prison" for the worst of the worse! I was being observed how I protected myself here, and what I could do, to transmit Light into this darkness. Sometimes we are sent there to assist and bring hope, so that one day even they can rejoin the way upwards towards the Light."

CHAPTER IV – THE ASTRAL PLANE

General Statements

Also called the astral light, the plane of glamour, illusion and emotions.

This is what the Greeks called Hades or underworld and Christianity the purgatory or intermediate state. There are many other names for it.

Today, the ignorant believe that only what our five senses can detect is real. Science tells us that only five to six percent of the matter in this universe is visible and can be measured by them. All else they call Dark Matter and Dark Energy. The Ancient Wisdom has held for eons that this unseen matter is astral and mental and even finer matter on higher planes. (See my chart on page 6)

Astral matter is fluid and in its original state it was pure astral energy directed via the Solar Logos* into our planetary life. Since humans developed the solar plexus chakra and became astral - emotional beings during Atlantean times, we have shaped this matter into every conceivable form.

Every emotion and thoughts are instantly given here a form out of astral elemental** matter. We are told that when humanity has evolved away from its emotional makeup, the astral plane will disappear. This might be thousands of years in the future.

*Logos: Greek for "The Word" or "God." The One in Whom we live and move and have our being. The Logos of our Solar system.

**Elemental life forms on the path of involution, downwards into the mineral kingdom; Nature-spirits or sprites. The esoteric usage, however, means beings who are beginning a course of evolutionary growth, and who therefore are in the elemental states of their growth.

The astral plane is a tremendously dynamic world. Rapid travel within this environment is only limited by the quality of vibrational matter and consciousness within your makeup. There is a constant movement of humans being drawn "up" towards the mental plane by the Soul and the "downward" move towards a new incarnation.

The consciousness of some of the domesticated, beloved pets and more evolved animals can be here for many months in their astral bodies. As we bestow love upon our pets, we provide them with the emotional material to refine and strengthen their astral body. Some might even overshadow a living, physical offspring or one of the same species and merge into its body. A few are already individualized but must wait for the door to the human kingdom to be opened again in a very far, distant future.

People arriving here have not changed in character or intellect in the slightest. Thy bring with them the same likes and dislikes, hate and love, sorrows, opinions and hang-ups. That death is "the universal leveler" is total nonsense.

The teaching by some religions that the departed should wait within the ground "until the angel blows the trumpet of resurrection" is causing some believers to substantially delay advancement while hovering in their etheric shell next to the corpse. Not a pretty sight to a sensitive onlooker and wasted time for the one who lost the physical body. Much confusion ensues when they finally arrive in the astral world.

The Many Life Forms

Many other life forms can be observed here. Remember that we share this planet with at least five other streams of life we know of, each of these having a huge number of forms moving through the astral and mental planes. (See next image) Some of these are the elemental and the deva (Angel) kingdoms in their enormous scores of forms. Others are nature-spirits of many different kinds and classes. In eons to come they might enter a future humanity similar to our own. Like most inhabitants in the astral plane, they are able to assume any shape at will.

THE EVOLUTION OF LIFE

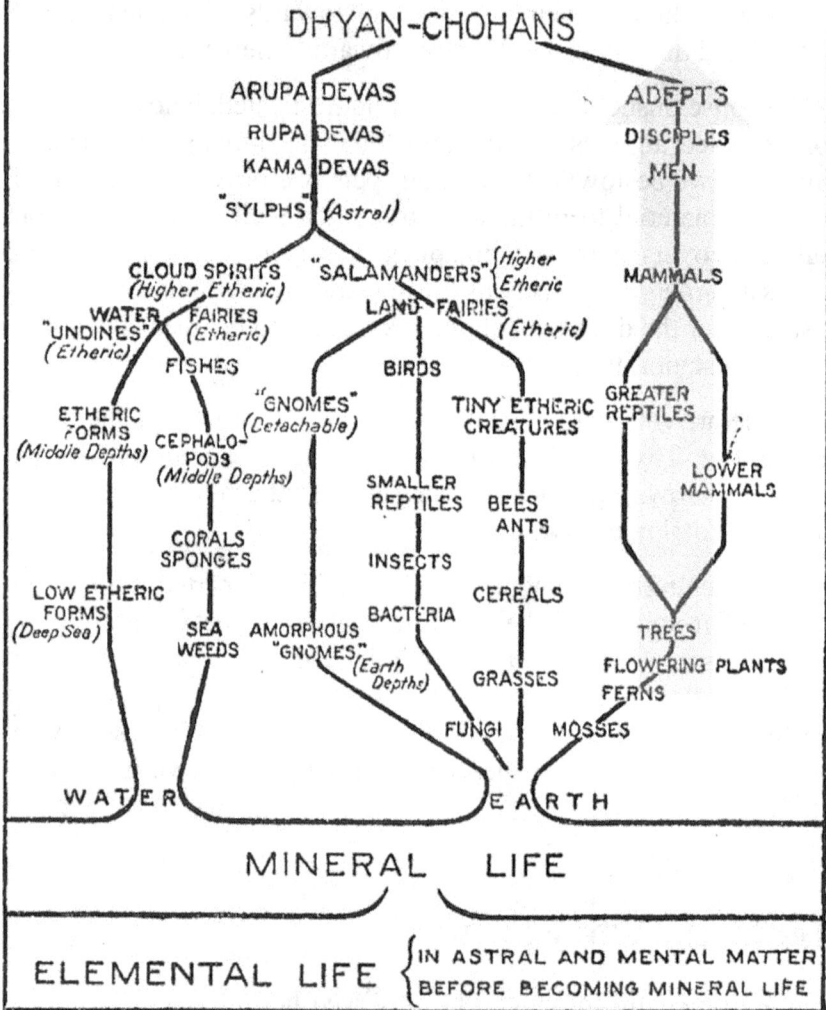

DHYAN-CHOHANS

ARUPA DEVAS   ADEPTS

RUPA DEVAS   DISCIPLES

KAMA DEVAS   MEN

"SYLPHS" (Astral)

CLOUD SPIRITS   "SALAMANDERS" {Higher Etheric}   MAMMALS
(Higher Etheric)

WATER FAIRIES   LAND FAIRIES
"UNDINES" (Etheric)   (Etheric)
(Etheric)

FISHES   BIRDS

"GNOMES"   TINY ETHERIC   GREATER
ETHERIC   (Detachable)   CREATURES   REPTILES
FORMS   CEPHALO-
(Middle Depths)   PODS
(Middle Depths)   LOWER
     SMALLER   MAMMALS
     REPTILES   BEES
       ANTS
CORALS
SPONGES   INSECTS

LOW ETHERIC   CEREALS
FORMS   BACTERIA
(Deep Sea)   SEA   AMORPHOUS   TREES
   WEEDS   "GNOMES" (Earth
      Depths)   GRASSES   FLOWERING PLANTS
               FERNS
      FUNGI   MOSSES

WATER   EARTH

MINERAL LIFE

ELEMENTAL LIFE { IN ASTRAL AND MENTAL MATTER
BEFORE BECOMING MINERAL LIFE

WE SHARE THIS PLANET WITH FIVE OTHER LIFE-STREAMS EVOLVING PARALLEL TO US.

There are also countless artificial forms created and imbued by human's thought and emotions. They seem semi-intelligent and mirror frequently Men's idols. You might find a hundred Elvis Presley here. Thought forms of fans build from elemental substance. They will disappear via attrition unless sustained by human thought.

An occasional appearance of those Adepts and other highly evolved Beings who mastered the human condition many years ago and normally reside on much higher planes of vibration, can be seen here. They temporarily create bodies on this and other planes to do work as required.

Here in the astral world, you might observe the selfish, dark forces of humanity and their pupils. Here, and in the four lower sub-planes of the mental plane they wage war against those forces of Love and selflessness. From here the dark forces drive their negative influence downwards into the physical realm via two major tools - the greedy economic situation and religious confusion and hatreds. This is why we have on Earth, right now, such chaotic, fragmented thinking prevalent in politics, religion, economics, social, education and philosophical areas. More, I don't want to say about these forces of darkness, since just thinking about them may attract their attention. Humanity will in spite of today's chaos and division come out of this stronger and more unified!

Outside of these mentioned, there are two other great evolutions using this planet whom we are not given any information about. These we will likely never encounter.

Our emotions right now have a substantial effect on the astral world's content. An example would be the very positive, highly emotion provoking show by Oprah Winfrey which started in 1986 and ran for 24 seasons. Large areas of the astral world were wiped out via the viewer's emotions and restructured instantly by the up to 26 to 42 million viewers each week! We do not create new astral elemental matter but only attract, concentrate and shape it primarily via our emotions and feelings!

"We can't become what we need to be by remaining what we are."

Oprah Winfrey

The Astral World Visualized

The astral plane has almost infinite levels of astral matter, containing from the grossest to the very finest. From the lowest denizens below the surface of Earth, to the most refined, bordering on the lowest mental plane. It is mostly the vibrational quality of the emotional matter (energy) we build into our astral bodies during physical life and the circumstances of our passing over, that will determine the level we initially end up in.

Notice where I placed earth-bound, bad persons and suicides and very evil persons. Remember, none of these have physical bodies any more.

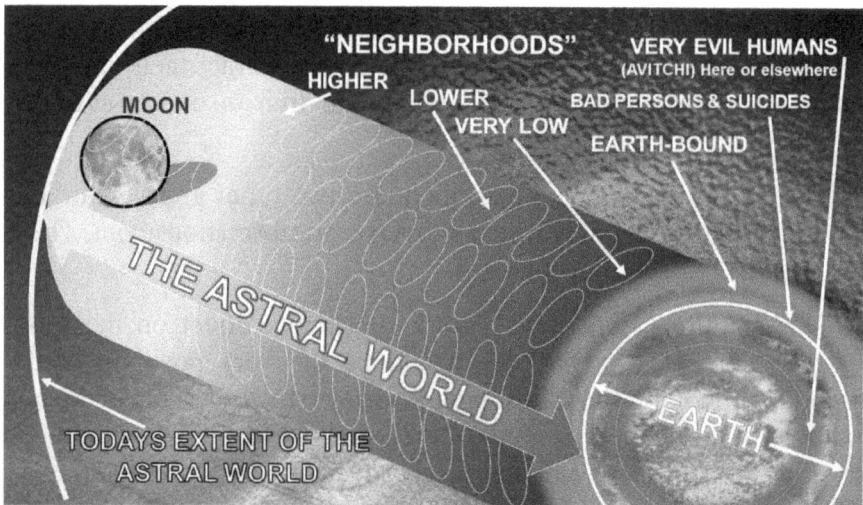

Imagine these "Neighborhoods" extending in <u>every</u> direction around the planet. Each of these attract groups of people sharing similar likes of music, art, sports, religion, etc. ... and hence share comparable QUALITY of consciousness and astral matter in their makeup.

It must be understood that nothing here is static. As you live-out and lose interest in whatever you were into, that astral matter is shed and you rise into the next higher "neighborhood" or sub-plane. It is like a child discarding a simple toy for a more complex one.

As nobler and spiritual your desire and emotions are, as more refined the astral matter making up your astral body is. Finer matter vibrates at a higher rate and when sequentially grosser matter is discarded, the consciousness of the person within it shifts into a higher vibration and sub-plane.

Dreams:

The astral world is where a person, still in a physical body, goes after putting his or her body to sleep. Some will bring back vague and fragmented images upon awakening and call it a dream. But while there and if trained to see clearly, it is so much more real and vivid to them than this physical life can be.

BRINGING BACK DISTORTED DREAMS.

Most of us are awake in the astral plane during sleep of our physical body but we have not fully "turned our senses outwards" to that plane. We have not learned to use the astral senses which employ the entire surface of the astral vehicle. Hence, we bring back into our physical brain only partial and distorted images from our experiences there.

Because this is the emotional plane, the beginner should pay special attentions to the emotional content of the "dream."

Nature again, provided us with protection and for good reasons. There is a "barrier" between our etheric body and the astral body we call the "etheric web". It consists of a single layer of atoms and a special type of energy (Prana) and its purpose is to prevent an unhindered view into the astral world until we have adequately evolved our consciousness. This protective web is "hardened" by smoking and alcohol and can "break" due to use of drugs and excessive alcohol.

This is what can happen to alcoholics when in the state of delirium tremens. The web becomes defective and the poor person's view is extended into the lowest levels of the astral planes. A horrendous sight unfolds before them.

Hearing on the astral plane is commonly called clairaudience. Many are more restricted in their communications just as they are in the physical. Since all sensing is done using the surface of the entire astral form, the range of sounds and sight are much further extended and one can see into the ultra-violet as well as into the infra-red spectrum. When focused rightly onto an astral body, the aura can be a brilliant play of colors.

Do you see now how confusing the astral world can be to new arrivals? This is one reason why "nature" kindly removes a certain amount of "critical faculties" from the average new-comer. This is caused by losing the physical brain that works with a part of the mind that continuously asks questions. This is the rationalizing faculty of the physical plane brain and its etheric counterpart.

CHAPTER V – LIFE IN THE ASTRAL PLANE

Elimination

The stage of "Elimination" is the process by which persons "live out" and eliminate those lower emotional vibrations and astral matter from their vehicles via attrition. We constantly shed the outer coverings of the astral body, just as we shed cells that line the surfaces of our physical body (epithelial cells). First, we shed the grosser and then finer matter. When all of the astral matter is discarded (lived out), the "second death" occurs and the person moves into the mental plane.

I describe the elimination of glamor and all the negative emotional baggage in great detail in my free video *"Personality Integration & Introduction to Meditation."* There, I show you three methods by which you can eliminate this burden <u>now</u>.

General Statements

The same basic rule applies to all people, but the experience differs in each case. Just like the physical body consists of various densities of solids, liquids, gases and etheric matter, so does the astral body consist of many variations of astral matter.

We determine the "vibrational quality" we build into our physical bodies via the food we eat, the environment we live in and the way we think, etc. ... The same way we decide the astral matter we build into our astral body via our emotions: hate, love, jealousy, kindness, spirituality or evil, etc. ....

The average stay here is twenty to thirty years our physical time but there are many exceptions. As less the person is attached to physical earth-life and relations left behind, as shorter his stay might be in the astral realm. This could be as short as just minutes, hours or a few days. Some advanced persons and much less emotional people like disciples and initiates may bypass the astral plane altogether by quickly shedding their astral body. Much depends directly on the amount and quality of astral matter that makes up the astral body. Here, less gross matter is better.

And again, I must emphasize the fact that what you do here while still in the physical body, will determine the quality and duration of your experience in the after-life! The seeds you have sown here, you will harvest on astral and mental and higher levels later.

"For sweetest things turn sourest by their deeds;
Lilies that fester smell far worse than weeds."

Shakespeare
from Sonnet 94

THE SEEDS YOU HAVE SOWN HERE, YOU WILL HARVEST LATER.

The Tunnel Experience:

After shedding the physical body, many people will experience moving through a tunnel towards a bright light to stand before an exalted being, a welcoming light, or a "Being of Light." From my personal experience I can assure you that this brief contact is a life-changing event!

It has a very definite personality and the love and the warmth which emanate from this being is absolute! This is in most, if not in all cases the moment of direct Soul contact. This is due to the fact that even in the most ignorant and undeveloped person, the moment of complete restitution (death) is noticed by the Soul.

Many people having had a "near death experience," report communications from *"this Being of Light."* Some report receiving the message that it is not yet their time, and to return to their physical body. There are thousands of reported near-death experiences supporting this fact.

Some report being greeted by friends and family members who died before. But remember, the average stay here is about twenty to thirty years our time. During and after this time, many of those you have known moved on to higher levels of the astral or even into the mental plane. What we understand by time here is nonexistent once we lose our physical brain.

This "tunnel" experience I consider to be more like an elevator ride. As you rise from the physical into the astral world in your body made up of astral and mental matter, you should get off on the floor (level or cell) you belong on. This is the natural law and best for you.

As you rise, you might see scenes on lower levels go by. **Do not linger regardless of how familiar or interesting they might appear!** As explained previously, the astral world has many cells or "neighborhoods" and one of these is just right for you. So, let the "quality" of your makeup carry you where you are supposed to be.

"In fact, in this model of death, that part of the journey would correspond to a high-speed crossing through a number of intermediary levels in which the (generally untrained) consciousness of the dying man has better not to "loiter on the way", lest he should have dangerous encounters with the tremendous powers lurking in this astral zone, in the form of unchecked energies and alluring, horrific pictures defying all imagination."

From the writings of Helena P. Blavatsky

Purely Emotional and Emotional-Mental Persons

This area of the astral plane "holds prisoner" the many people who die while their major reaction to life is that of desire, of wishful thinking and of emotional consciousness. These people have well developed emotional bodies but less evolved mental vehicles. They are still the vast majority of humans and initially have only access to the astral plane.

The statements below also apply to persons having achieved some balance between their emotions and mental focus. All are committed to a period of elimination within the illusory, emotional world of this plane.

Most moral, emotional people discover themselves upon the astral plane, clothed in a shell of astral matter with whatever mental substance was accumulated. They resemble in shape, size, age and clothing just how they think of themselves. Many look substantially younger than their physical body they just discarded.

We have to constantly remind ourself that all these outer forms are no more that tools that we the Soul, we the Spirit, have acquired to express ourselves and learn in.

Many arrivals seem to have lost their critical faculties, the constantly questioning and challenging mind we experience in the physical brain. Some people fall asleep after permanently vacating their physical body only to wake up here, and in the right area where they belong.

Upon arrival here, the person would describe this world as an absolute reality and solidity. However, initially they find what they perceive very confusing. Can you imagine focusing on an object and seeing all sides of it simultaneously? Or smelling a rose from across the room? Something desired and focused upon will come about. Desire and emotions here will shape everything.

FOCUS UPON A ROSE AND FEED IT LOVE. SEE HOW IT GROWS!

A fair depiction of the astral world was attempted by a wonderful 2002 movie named *"What Dreams May Come"*, starring Robin Williams, Cuba Gooding Jr. and Annabella Sciorra. ISBN 9780783277547 and you find it on Netflix, HBO, etc. … I highly recommend it. However, suicide is not depicted accurately nor can the individual determine the time for incarnation.

The people arriving here have lost some of their acute awareness of their body's needs like hunger, bowel movement, pain, etc. Arthritic knees, a missing limb, the need for sleep, the illness they died of are gone. Nature is kind! Many will not even realize that they lost their physical body. This is good, since the shock and confusion would be overwhelming for most.

But now we have gained besides those senses we were used to, several improvements on them, i.e., the colors are much more vivid, travel is rapid, no more pain, clearer perception, and so much more. Truly a fuller life. I refer you to many books available on the subject that explain people's activities and surroundings.

Here, your vehicle of consciousness is made up of many grades of exceedingly fine matter and looks just as you think of yourself (frequently younger). The astral body has all the sense organs like ears, eyes, nose, but we don't use these at all. Close observation will reveal that all types of the body's different quality particles are in constant motion and intermingle, and as mentioned before, we learn to use the entire body's surface as sense organs.

Here is something not often taught in esoteric schools:

Initially, the average, mostly emotional person entering the astral world will be able to see some or most of life within the various levels of this plane. But not too long a time passes before the matter of the astral body arranges itself in "onion-like" layers. The grossest matter on the outside and from there, finer and finer matter towards the center.

This is caused by our astral elemental trying to fight the dissolution of the astral body just as the physical elemental did during physical death! These elementals are those agents that make our physical, astral and mental bodies to last as long as is possible. Not necessarily a negative thing. Arranging of astral matter with the coarsest and grossest matter on the outside provides the greatest resistance to dissolution.

Since it is the outer layer that serves as the sense organs, the obvious consequence is that the person's senses become restricted to perceiving and interacting only with matter of that level or sub-plane. The person effected in such way is totally unconscious of the loss.

The astral elemental instinctively instills the fear of dying in the person and if given in to it, his or her movement towards higher planes will be seriously delayed or hindered. This can be avoided via certain knowledge and training. One is control over strong desire/emotions right now and trained focus. Remember that matter is energy and energy follow thought, especially in the astral and higher worlds!

And here again, it is via **attrition, living out** or **elimination** of the matter of a given sub-plane within your astral body that allows advancing into "higher," more refined areas of the astral realm.

The Integrated Persons

Persons with an integrated personality have reached a point of balance between mental and emotional focus and maturity that promotes logic and reason. These people have "freedom of the dual life," and find themselves within a well-developed astral and mental body which enables them to contact at will the higher levels of the astral plane and the lower levels of the mental plane.

They got to this point because they eliminated glamor, and a well-balanced mental body and mind govern their lives. Here are the many "good" intellectuals.

Life is more refined here and travel within these higher astral sub-planes is so much quicker. Here, observation of matter and even individual elements and atoms is possible. I recall "pulling" myself into and though the trunk of a tree only to find myself quickly recognizing less and less of what I saw. At the end of that amplified vision only strings of colored energy remained.

These persons use two methods of **elimination**, dramatically reducing the time they spent in the astral world:

❖ They eliminate the astral body by means of the growing desire for mental life. They withdraw gradually and steadily into the mental body, and the astral body esoterically "drops away" and finally disappears like fog exposed to sunlight.

❖ They are attracted towards the soul and the more advanced people shatter the astral body by an act of the human will. Knowledge of these matters will greatly assist this. This "upwards" movement is encouraged via the love of the Soul and the energies coming from the Monad (our Spirit) via the Sutratma.

The Undeveloped Persons

Humans, just as every member of every kingdom came about with an equal potential to evolve towards something much greater! However, this does not mean that we, the individuals of the human kingdom incarnate equally in consciousness and experience.

Here we are talking about young, unevolved Souls, mostly incarnating in simple people. These too are of equal importance since one could argue that the first grade in school could be equally important as high school.

One vitally important point we should not lose sight of is, that it is the Soul that builds the bodies for its personality consciousness. These bodies and personality are the best the Soul can, and is allowed to manifest at this point in Its evolution.

The astral body of an undeveloped person appears vague and shapeless in outline. It is only with the growth of the intellect that the outlines become more defined.

For the unevolved, death is literally a sleep and a forgetting. Where the mind is undeveloped, the inner person finds him/herself practically smothered in an envelope of astral matter, immersed in the astral plane and gently dreaming of the physical life just left behind.

Those people drift at their level of the astral plane, like wrapped within a cocoon, unconscious to the outside world. They should not be disturbed and no attempt to wake them should be made.

The Soul who is unevolved withdraws Its life-force and almost immediately reincarnates again via a new personality. The personality does not advance into the mental plane, because there is very little for the Soul to grow by. But not all is lost. Whatever positive skills and attributes were gained are stored and converted within the permanent atoms as vibrational qualities, benefitting the personality in the next life to come.

Earth-bound Good and Bad People

Just like with suicides and only in very rare cases, earth-bound people here become so desperate for contact with physical earth-life to undo whatever stranded them here, that they succeed in possessing incarnate people who are physically/etherically feeble and intellectually weak. Grave karmic consequences are the result!

But, all will sooner or later rise to the level in the plane their makeup of astral and mental matter dictates. All those diversions and hindrances will wear out and fall away. Whatever held them back will have resolved itself and children will have grown up. Their payment for this is the extra anguish, pain and time they are spending in the astral.

LETTING GO.

The condition and duration of their stay within this lower astral level varies widely from person to person. It strengthens the hold of the astral elemental on the person's astral body, making it harder to overcome its resistance later. From here they will find their area in the astral world as described earlier.

Suicides, Victims of Sudden and Violent Death

In cases like heart-attacks etc., the normal experience is not unpleasant - varying from near unconsciousness to vivid but dream-like memories of earth. Because of the shock of this type of transition, they tend to be in the lower areas of the astral for a short time, reliving again and again what they were into when passing.

Violent Death Victims

I am reminded of such occurrence in my earlier years. A drag-race took place on our road in the early morning hours and one of the cars slammed at a very high speed into a power pole right outside our house. The young driver was thrown clear and I found him leaning against our wall. Before an ambulance could arrive, and as I held his hand, he passed over.

Just as we prepared to settle down to resume our sleep, the young man appeared in his very powerful etheric body in front of us. Frantically clinging to life, he had withdrawn some matter from his physical body.

His demeanor was that of anger and bewilderment. He had no idea that he had lost his physical body and blamed us for stopping the race. We tried to explain to him but when that failed, we projected love and Light towards him and he disappeared.

So, it is with many sudden death occurrences. Many of us are actually called upon nightly to work in the astral plane to assist such victims by explaining to them their new found environment and what to do next. In virtually all such cases there exists confusion and the lack of knowledge that they lost their physical body. Those good and more spiritual people having no affinity to this lower plane, tend to fall into a pleasant dream state while they slowly move into the higher level, they belong in.

And again, many, having passed over, have lost a certain amount of their critical faculties. That too is nature's way to limit the shock. Only when you ask them questions like, "When did you last eat, when did you last go to the bathroom, why do you look younger and why do you feel no pain?", will a glimmer of understanding slowly come to them.

Soldiers Dying in Battle

The continuity in what they were into is especially pronounced with soldiers dying in battle. They tend to continue fighting their enemy for some time. Their patriotic feelings, panic of the moment and hate of their enemy will take a long time to wear out. Not a pleasant scene to watch.

But this situation will also wear out sooner or later, and they too will find their right place within the astral world.

Suicides

They are fully conscious in the lower astral plane. During this time, they suffer according to the motive for taking their own lives. If their deed was from a high, unselfish motive (seldom), then their period of consciousness is not intolerable and sometimes even rewarding. If the motive was selfish or cowardly, they will suffer remorse and regret amplified many times and for a long time. The karmic consequences are substantial and could produce damage for lifetimes to come.

In all cases, sooner or later these energies wear out and the persons takes up their place within the astral plane determined by their qualities of astral and mental matter. This might take years for some. However, each person in these groups must remain in the astral world as long as their normal lifespan would have been in the physical body.

Earth-bound Entities, Addicted Heavily to Drugs or Alcohol

I need to briefly mention the type of earth-bound people who are for a while bound to the astral plane lowest to the physical earth plane. Many of these people having committed "suicide" with drugs or alcohol, are attracted to bars, drug dens, and alcoholics and drug addicts still in physical bodies while they sleep.

Here is what my teacher Dr. Douglas M. Baker M.D. observed in the astral:

"...the fate of those alcoholics who take their own lives only to find themselves still earthbound by their attraction towards alcohol and its fumes.

In that work,* I showed that one of the main causes of both, alcoholism and the difficulties experienced by those trying to recover from it, to "dry out" or to win their way back through convalescence to normality, was the constant vampirism upon the individual by astral entities who had once been themselves alcoholics.

"In an alcoholic coma, it is possible for astral vampirism to occur because in this state the liver, busily metabolising the alcohol, cannot separate entirely from the astral body and this linkage point provides an attractive area for astral entities to "sip" at the astro-physical fumes of alcohol in this region."

Life after Death, by Dr. Douglas M. Baker
Alcoholism - The Hidden Significance
by Dr. Douglas M. Baker

Needless to say, that their actions will have karmic consequences for life-times to come.

But like with almost all conditions here, this too will wear out sooner or later and they can move higher into the astral world to live out their time. Many must forego their ascent into the mental planes.

Another quotation:

"The third "division" is of an intensely vivid nature. Extreme delirium carries the patient to this plane. In delirium tremens the sufferer passes to this and to the one above it. Lunatics are often conscious on this plane, where they see terrible visions..."

"The fourth "division", the worst of the astral plane .... Hence come the images that tempt; images of drunkards ... impelling others to drink; images of all vices inoculating men with the desire to commit crimes. Extreme delirium tremens is on this plane."

The Theosophist, March 1931,
by H. P. Blavatsky.

THE FOURTH DIVISION OF THE ASTRAL PLANE.
HORRENDOUS IMAGES CAN BE PART OF DELIRIUM TREMENS.

According to one of H.P. Blavatsky's masters:

"No man dies insane or unconscious, ... " "... Even a madman or one in a fit of delirium tremens will have his instance of perfect lucidity at the moment of death, though unable to say so to those present."

Children and Babies

Here is what a highly trained observer writes about children dying of a disease or accident and arriving in the astral world:

> *"Where a child's astral body is more definite in shape and somewhat integrated, survival as an independent being is possible. Usually, they have to be carefully led through a process of maturing emotionally, which is accompanied by the integration of the astral body."*

> *"In this way they may grow into adults, usually of an extraordinary refinement. Such children are watched over by guardians in the astral world who are carefully selected for this purpose. From here all normal rules apply."*

By Charles W. Leadbeater

Aspirants, Disciples and Initiates

For many aspirants and all disciples and initiates, physical death is an immediate entrance into a sphere of service they are accustomed to in the astral and mental planes. They will go directly, and in full consciousness from the physical plane into the mental plane.

While the third initiates were at will, conscious in the astral and mental levels while still in the physical body, the former two might have been only fully conscious there while their physical body was asleep.

They will immediately oppose the astral/desire elemental, to retain all astral body's particles intermingled and in free motion, allowing sight into all levels of the astral and lower four sub-planes of the mental plane. Here, most of them can use telepathy to communicate with others.

Now, all three groups have access within the astral and mental planes to work and learn within their Master's ashram without sleep, much clearer thinking, and so much quicker.

Special circumstances permit forgoing the rewards of the "heaven world" (renunciation) and a quick return into reincarnation to continue the work. These special circumstances require approval by the Master and the Soul and are depending on the person's karma, equipment and world needs. More on this later. However, per Charles W. Leadbeater this might require the person to remain in the astral world while waiting for the right body or circumstances to become available.

Chapter Conclusion

All those who lived their required span of time here, have used up or worn out via attrition the old behavioral and emotional patterns.

My purpose in this book is not to talk about the Monad, but here I must inject something. During the person's journey through the astral, and later through the mental plane, the attracting love of the Soul played an important part. But also remember this:

**What the personality is to the Soul –
the Soul is to the Monad.**

It is also the Monad's pure spiritual power, that draws a person after physical death "upwards" into the Soul.

The longing for something higher increases and the person undergoes the "second death." There is no struggle to stay in the astral world since all the lower desires and matter have been "lived out" and shed. Only the most noble feelings and finest astral matter remain and now even this falls away and the person becomes fully conscious in the lower levels of the mental plane.

What they leave behind is an astral shell, a weak copy of the original owner. These in time fade away and all particles are returned to their source. These "shades" as we call them, still have a faint connection to its previous owner.

Before they fade out, it is these shades that at times are contacted by psychics. By doing so, some mediums can do some karmic damage to its former owner, perhaps even for lives to come! The original owner has departed and this is why in seances the shades display no original thoughts. All actual consciousness and intelligence have left this shade. Many "mental" mediums unknowingly get their information from the aura of the sitter (customer) who requested the contact with the diseased person. These shades are also very infrequently sized upon by despicable black magic forces and temporarily used for their evil purpose. All these remnants are bound to disintegrate sooner or later.

CHAPTER VI – THE MENTAL PLANE

General Description

Also called the Heaven-world by Christians, Shamayim by Jews, Jannah by Muslims, Devachan by the Wisdom, the plane of illusion, etc. I prefer to just call it the mental plane and define life in its sub-planes more accurately. Further, I would like to reserve the title of Devachan to the third mental sub-plane and those above that in vibrational quality. The over-used words like "bliss" and "eternity" should not be so glibly applied.

Very briefly, **bliss:** what joy is to us on the physical and astral plane, is bliss on the four lower sub-planes of the mental plane. The "strength" of this "ecstasy" also depends on the personality's spirituality, which sub-plane and many other factors. However strong it might be, it is no more than a candle is to the Sun when the purified consciousness, the "I, the Thinker" finally merges into the Soul on the third sub-plane and the old personality disappears! We must not think of bliss here as reward but rather as result of the earth-life. As smaller the gains brought, as shorter the stay here!

Eternity: another word pandered around by religions which most people cannot comprehend. Some religions advocate that after death and if we have lived up to a certain standard of morality and accepted certain theological beliefs, which differ with the different Churches in the West, we shall go to heaven and live there for eternity. Just what we do in heaven while spending the countless millions of years there is not stated. Presumably there is some sort of progress, but just what this means is not defined.

Here, the teaching of reincarnation and continued refinement and advancement with underlined future potential, provides a much more logical argument.

The mental plane just as the astral world, is divided into seven sub-planes. The four lower sub-planes we number four through seven and the three higher sub-planes, one through three (counting from "above.") In these planes the matter is even finer, and vibrationally faster than in the astral plane. Man's Soul resides on the third mental sub-plane. Higher vibration also means higher energy.

As you can assume by now, as closer we get to the abode of the Soul, as more refined, spiritual and bathed in more intense bliss the consciousness becomes. All the while, we learn and benefit from our processing the recently closed physical life.

PLANE	Subplanes
Higher Mental	1
	2
	SOUL 3
Lower Mental	4
	5
	6
	7

The Sub-divisions of the Mental Plane.

Just like in the astral sub-planes, here too, each sub-plane accommodates many levels of increasingly finer and finer matter. And with that, more and more advanced people. Particles of matter in the lowest mental sub-plane could be a million times smaller than in the highest astral sub-plane. Science is still far away from understanding that this mental and even finer matter on higher planes is what they named "Dark Energy." Astral matter they call "Dark Matter."

Why is the universe expanding at an <u>ever-increasing</u> rate? (A cosmological fact today.) Could it be that the "Dark Energy", the mental and higher cosmic planes are expanding because the universe is becoming more and more <u>self-conscious</u>? We call this "expansion of consciousness" and believe that this is occurring throughout the Cosmos, and at an ever-increasing rate!

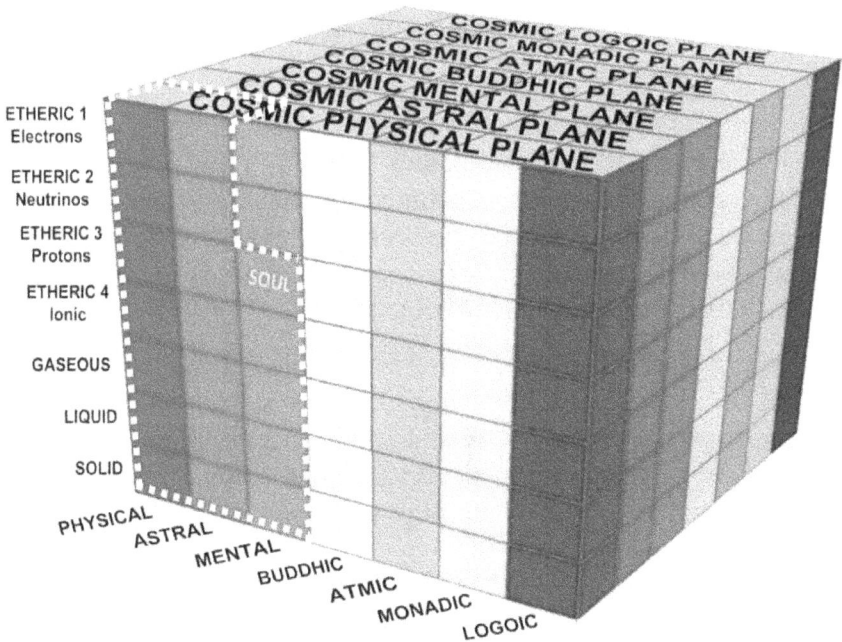

DIVISIONS OF ALL PLANES WITHIN OUR COSMOS

UNDERSTAND, THAT ALL THE PLANES OF MATTER/VIBRATION DEALT WITH IN THIS BOOK ARE OUTLINED IN WHITE DOTTED LINES!

We must remind ourselves that time and space as we know it on earth does not exist here, and sub-planes are only states of consciousness. The fineness and quality of the matter we build into our mental unit determines at what level of vibration we place ourself after astral "death."

The reader must clearly understand that the words "higher" and "lower" have nothing to do with location. However, C. W. Leadbeater, a very trained observer, told us that the mental plane interpenetrates the astral world and extends even further into space than the astral planes.

Virtually all people's mental body while still in the physical world, exist in the lower section, sub-planes four through seven. Extremely few, while still incarnate, can become fully conscious here and bring back memory of this into the physical brain. Remember, the term "plane" denotes a range or extent of some state of consciousness, fineness of matter and its rate of vibration.

It is here where mental telepathy is possible between two or more individuals. Here the concrete mind of man resides and from here thought-forms originate. When fully conscious here, no misunderstanding between persons can come about. Every thought, motivation and knowledge about the subject at hand is laid open to two or more conversing people.

Thinking of, or visualizing a place will take you there virtually instantaneously.

On higher levels of the mental plane, the long line of past lives can be reviewed and karma still to be worked out becomes known.

Describing any scene in this level is virtually impossible. Many attempts have been made by every religion, every prophet, books and poetry written. Every time the scene was described, it seems totally based on the belief and consciousness of the reporter. It is even harder to attempt to describe the unfettered and blissful state one finds themselves in.

A Teacher's Description

"Do not complain and cry and pray, but open your eyes and see. The light is all about you, if you would only cast the bandage from your eyes and look. It is so wonderful, so beautiful, so far beyond what any man has dreamt of or prayed for, and it is forever and forever."

The Soul of a People, page 163,
by the Buddhist teacher.

"To take one only of many possible examples of our difficulties, it would seem as though on this mental plane space and time were non-existing, for events which down here take place in succession and at widely separated places, appear to be occurring simultaneously and at the same point."

The Devachanic Plane, page 8
by C. W. Leadbeater.

CHAPTER VII – MENTAL PLANE LIFE

Integration

Just as giving up the physical body is named **redemption** and living-out the astral body **elimination,** the next cleansing is called **integration**.

This entails ridding the mental body of all that the Soul cannot grow by. Whatever spiritual quality may be left, is <u>integrated</u> into the Soul. And yes, we are now confronted with the end of the personality's existence. Only upon arriving here, does the more advanced person begin to be very dimly aware of this fact.

I must now reiterate the point I made so many times before; we are the "I", the "Thinker" within! The part of the Soul's consciousness It sent forth into the physical, astral and mental planes to become conscious and interact therein.

> "... *The subjective and mystical "death of the personality," This is a phrase indicating the transfer of the focus for the distribution of energy from the personality (a definite centre of force) to the soul (another definite centre)."*
>
> *A treatise on the Seven Rays, vol III,*
> *Esoteric Astrology*, by Alice A. Bailey

The Purely Emotional - Undeveloped Persons

> *"After a long process of attrition in the astral world, is left standing free within an embryonic mental vehicle, and this period of semi-mental life is exceedingly brief and is brought to an end by the soul who suddenly "directs his eye to the waiting one," and of the power of that directed potency instantaneously reorients the individual kamic man to the downward path of rebirth."*

Esoteric Healing,
A Treatise on the Seven Rays,
vol IV, p 498, by Alice A. Bailey

In this case, the Soul can gain very little to grow its qualities. However, the additional attributes like mechanical skills, adaptability, emotional steadiness, mental agility, etc., are not lost by any type of person! These qualities are also stored as "vibrational qualities" and faculties in the permanent atoms and benefit the Soul in Its next incarnation.

The Balanced, Average Good Persons

First, remember this; just as during an incarnation we are attracting emotional matter and energy into and around our astral body, we did the same with our mental body. What we call "emotional glamour" in the astral body, we call "illusional, false thinking" in the mental body. These accumulations I describe in detail in my video "*Journey into Consciousness*" and again, in "*Personality Integration and Introduction to Meditation*" In this video I give you three methods by which you can eliminate your emotional and mental negative baggage.

Initially, all people clothed in whatever mental bodies they build while in the physical world arrive in the lower section of the mental plane. Almost each one has matter within the mental body that belongs to more than one sub-plane.

On this planet there are as many unique combinations of these mental accumulations as there are people. From the primitive to the most highly advanced thinkers, virtually all arrive here in the mental plane. All of them have eliminated all their emotional "baggage" but are still carrying with them misapprehensions, false thinking and concretized thought-forms. These attributes must be eliminated (lived out) after arrival in the lower four sub-planes of the mental plane.

Since man's thoughts are so much more powerful in the mental plane, we find lots of artificial elementals imitating humanity's idols. They persist substantially longer here than in the astral plane. Those are the thought-forms of stars and even family created by people here, and those still in incarnation.

Upon losing the astral body, most people become unconscious and after a while, they gradually awaken in their mental vehicle. The first sensation is that of bliss and then slowly they become aware of their new body. This process is very enjoyable and can take a few minutes to a substantially longer time. Most will find their surroundings very pleasant and populated by images of self-created people and the environment they have known.

Here, the persons live entirely in the world of their own thoughts, still fully identifying themself with the personality in the life which was not too long ago left behind. Now, they pursue interests they had while in the physical, all positive and so much less hampered than ever before. Their state is that of happiness and bliss and the length and intensity is governed only by their own mental makeup and thoughts while in incarnation. Negative karma is suspended until their next physical incarnation.

This process of purging for some might take from a few days up to twenty-five years our time. What helps with this process is that their illusions, concretized thought-forms and false thinking left their emotional force behind in the astral world.

I would like to refer the reader to the books referenced, to explain in more detail the personal life of people within these lower mental sub-planes.

Just as the physical and astral elementals tried to preserve their existence, so does the mental elemental; one more factor determining the duration and experience each person can have at this point.

Here, are a few valuable sample attributes to have, and also those that will prevent the person from entering the mental world:

Helpful when entering, unselfishness in:

❖ Affection for family or friends.

❖ Religious devotion of love and gratitude, and empathy for all life. This takes the person into the sixth or even into a higher mental sub-plane.

❖ Love and good will poured out <u>and seeking nothing in return</u>.

What cannot enter:

❖ The exacting, **selfish** love, a possessive kind of passion that demands to be loved back. "I will love you as long you love me!"

❖ Religious devotees, whose primary thought is how they may save their own miserable "souls."

Any selfish feelings are of astral quality and forces the personality to remain in the astral realm. These attributes will never rise above the astral plane. Here, and just in general terms, the dark forces mentioned earlier have only temporary and limited powers because of selfishness being their primary motivation.

Now, the Soul takes greater and greater interest in the person approaching the higher planes.

> *"The freed consciousness then moves into the mental world, a world in which form has practically vanished and in which symbol and image have become paramount. In the mental world the last of our personality behavioral patterns, reflexes and memories are slowly discarded, and after a period of twenty years, another "death" occurs as the last vestiges of man's form structure are dispensed with. The residual consciousness — really the spiritual essence of all experiences of the previous life — leaves behind the mental unit and anchors itself to the mental permanent atom in the heaven world.*

" …… and while the consciousness (the person) very peacefully broods over the spiritual events of the last life, the soul extracts the remaining elements of Atma (Spiritual Will), Buddhi (Wisdom-Love) and Manas (Active Intelligence) which, directed into itself, stir further the opening of its petals of consciousness.

"….. This process usually takes about 1,000 years in the heaven state, depending on the Ray of the soul. Some require somewhat less, usually about 700 years. It should, however, be emphasised here that there are many, many exceptions to these basic rules."

Life After Death, by Dr. Douglas M. Baker
(in brackets added by author)

Today the stay in devachan is somewhat shorter because of the vast increase in available human physical bodies during the last one hundred years to reincarnate in.

The Integrated and Spiritual Persons

Many intelligent, balanced and more advanced thinkers find on the **fourth** mental sub-plane opportunity to continue further learning and working out philanthropic ideas to help others.

C. W. Leadbeater placed people rising into the fourth sub-plane into these main groups:

❖ Unselfish pursuit of spiritual knowledge.

❖ High philosophic or scientific thought, literary or artistic ability exercised for unselfish purposes, and service for the sake of service.

❖ Some aspirants, disciples and those evolved scientists and religious intelligent people.

❖ Eager to learn from their master and teachers.

These are the result of advanced Souls. Many of these by now have realized that they are the "I", the "Thinker" within and the remaining mental sheath is just a tool. All illusion now has been discarded. They know that their knowledge gained is soon to be converted into faculties, wisdom and refinements to be used in lives to come.

> *"This person is inspirited by the Soul's intentions and has subordinated the mind to this purpose. When this point in evolution is attained, the person can then dissolve the last remaining vestiges of all desire by means of illumination. In the early stages of purely manasic or mental life, this is done through the illumination which knowledge brings and involves mainly the innate light of mental substance."*

> *".... when elimination is complete and the hour of soul contact eventuates and the manasic (mental) vehicle is in process of destruction, he (the person) becomes immediately aware of the future, for prediction is an asset of the soul consciousness and in this the man temporarily shares."*

> *"Therefore, past, present and future are seen as one; the recognition of the Eternal Now is gradually developed from incarnation to incarnation and during the continuous process of rebirth. This constitutes a state of consciousness (characteristic of the normal state of the advanced man) which can be called devachanic."*

> *Esoteric Healing, A Treatise on the Seven Rays,*
> *vol IV, p 497*, by Alice A. Bailey

The Aspirants, Disciples and Initiates

Having arrived here, they still have full access to the astral plane if required to work there. The desire of aspirants, disciples and initiates is to work off karma quickly and to liberate themself for service. With most, there is no desire for a period of rest on the fourth sub-plane or in devachan and they seek to work in their Master's ashram or to rapidly reincarnate.

Renouncing the reward of devachan and other options are possible depending on their development, certain laws, and the full concurrence of their Soul and their Master. The requestor must also fully know what he is forfeiting. This permission is not easily given since it sacrifices the Soul benefitting from the incarnation just closed.

The absorption of all that is positive within the personality is necessary to convert these into faculties and wisdom the Soul can grow by and to be available for the next incarnation. However, for the highly advanced person this should not slow down their progress.

As our consciousness expands and we can fully experience the higher mental planes, we begin to understand the lesser reality of the life on the planes below. The brilliance of color, the so much less hampered thought processes, the lesser or none existing gravity, pain-less-ness, and speed of travel will convince you more and more of the fact that the physical and astral realms are less real.

But if they decide to go into devachan:

> *The disciple now uses more occult methods, but upon these I may not here enlarge. The destruction of the mental body is no longer brought about by the destructive power of light itself, but is hastened by means of certain sounds, emanating from the plane of the spiritual will; these are recognised by the disciple, and permission to use them in their proper word-forms is given to him by some senior initiate within the Ashram or by the Master Himself, towards the close of the cycle of incarnation."*

> *Esoteric Healing, A Treatise on the Seven Rays,*
> vol IV, p 499, by Alice A. Bailey

Initiates and many of those who are rapidly developing intellectual capacities, tend to reincarnate quickly. These advanced Souls respond to the pull of interests, obligations and responsibilities already established upon the physical plane.

In my previous videos, Introduction to the Ancient Wisdom, Part III, *"Personality Integration and Introduction to Meditation,"* I stressed the importance of strengthening the Antahkarana and purifying the lower vehicles. Search and download from my website https://www.douglasbaker.org, part #6064 *"Extending the Channel to a Higher Level"* instructions for free. This work, and the instructions given in the book *"The Rainbow Bridge, Part I & II"*, will assist the ease and speed in which restitution, elimination and integration can occur for this group.

"Devachan is the fulfilling of all the unfulfilled spiritual hopes of the past incarnation, and an efflorescence (drawing out) of all the spiritual and intellectual yearnings of the past incarnation which in that past incarnation have not had an opportunity for fulfillment. It is a period of unspeakable bliss and peace for the human soul, until it has finished its rest time and stage of recuperation of its own energies...."

"In the devachanic state, the incarnating ego remains in the bosom of the Monad (or of the Monadic essence) in a state of the most perfect and utter bliss and peace, constantly reviewing, and improving upon in its own blissful imagination, all the unfulfilled spiritual and intellectual possibilities of the life just closed that its naturally creative faculties automatically suggest to the devachanic entity."

Occult Glossary, by G. de Purucker

Here in the third sub-plane, you also find those less evolved souls that function as group souls.* They overshadow the elemental kingdom on its way "downward" towards the physical plane, while others guide the evolution of the mineral, plant and animal kingdoms on its upward evolution towards human individualization.

Now, the human consciousness has finally entered its true home and the consciousness is ONE again. Here, in the third mental sub-plane, many billion human souls reside (one thousand-million is one billion). A very few, a small minority of these are to be found on sub-planes two and one. These are fully conscious of their domain and the directions and control of the next incarnating personality is so much more refined, truer and expressing high spirituality.

On the first sub-plane of the mental plane, we find the Masters of the Wisdom and Compassion, and their initiated students. Now the initiates know, that all these many incarnations are really just <u>one</u> life. They are fully conscious on the astral and mental planes below and can function on them.

* The younger Monads and Souls working in groups to direct the evolution of the lower kingdoms until human individualization. See *"The Jewel in the Lotus"*, p 93 - 97, by Douglas M. Baker.

Within the three higher mental sub-planes, we also find a vast host of visiting and descending life forms. One of these is the elemental essence on their way downwards towards the mineral kingdom. They greatly benefit by being used by our thoughts to create the wonderful colors and shapes upon the mental plane. There is also the deva kingdom but all of this lies outside the subject of this book.

Review and Being ONE Again

Here, is perhaps the right place to remind the reader once more, that we are not our bodies, not even our personality. We are the "I", the "Thinker within," the "Consciousness that is forever" who has now been purified and is a positive force and one with the Soul, experiencing true bliss. We are now aware of our past lives, the potential future, and know the needs and the plan for our next incarnation in a vague and general sense.

The purpose of our earthly life was to gather and express ever greater qualities like love, wisdom, intelligence, unselfishness, goodness, harmlessness, … etc. These are the qualities the Soul can grow by.

The long journey of redemption (physical death), elimination in the astral and integration in the mental planes, was to cleanse the portion of oneself (the personality) from all that, by which the Soul cannot grow.

Only the very best qualities gained can rise into the higher mental sub-planes where our true Being, the Soul within its causal body resides.

One earthly human body does not last long enough to bring the Soul's "Lotus" (its attributes & qualities) into full bloom. Hence, the Soul must incarnate and withdraw that part of itself again and again. Beautifying and growing its causal body and Self via this joining, absorption and integration of all the worth-while essence of its personality life just completed. The ancient wisdom tells us that this may take about 777 incarnations.

The image of the "Lotus" is only symbolic, but it helps us to visualize its growing qualities. In reality the Soul within its causal vehicle is a self-conscious, group-conscious and in potential a Logos-conscious entity. It is a vortex of force, twelve energies held together by the Will of the overshadowing Monad, our Spirit.

The causal body or Egoic egg is spheroidal in shape, and expands with each incarnation until it becomes a sphere of pulsating light of great beauty.

Now, having arrived at unity with the Soul, there is a total union of consciousness. Separation no longer exists and group-consciousness ensues. This is true self-realization and nirvanic bliss follows.

"The process of integration is dealing with the period wherein the liberated Soul again becomes conscious of itself as the Angel of the Presence and is reabsorbed into the world of souls, thus entering into a state of reflection".

Esoteric Healing
A Treatise on the Seven Rays
vol IV, p 433, by Alice A. Bailey

In all men lurks The Light; yet, in how few
Has it blazed forth, as rightfully it ought,
Illuming, from within, our fleshly lamp,
And kindling cosmic flame in nigh-brought souls!
Splendour of God, how few! And ours the blame;
For, ever, crassly, by routine and wrath,
We undiscerningly damp down and choke
The spark of God that glints in every child.
All children are, by nature, bits of God;
And God, if they but had their freedom, would
Unfold Himself in them, would burgeon forth
Tinting and moulding, till, as perfect flowers
They bloomed, fulfilled of loveliness unveiled.

Illuminant
Dr. Winslow Hall

CHAPTER VIII - REINCARNATION

Conclusion and the Reincarnation Cycle

It is preposterous to believe that one life span of seventy years would be sufficient for any of us to master the human kingdom and to evolve spiritually enough to function permanently in the kingdom of the Soul!

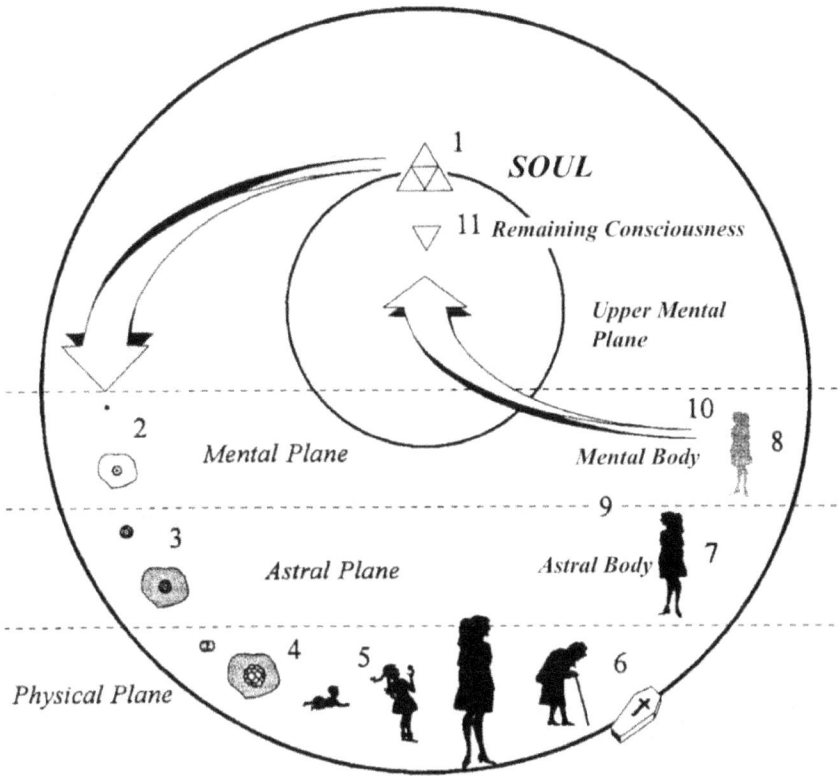

THE REINCARNATION CYCLE

The Soul's Journey
(Cyclo-spiritual Metamorphosis)

"Our drawing of the cyclic journey of man into and out of incarnation and his passage through the various states of the heaven world will serve to clarify the abstruse nature of the reincarnation process.

1. The soul on its own plane, feeling the urge of the 'Will-to-Be' once more, puts part of itself down into the mental plane.

2. In the mental plane the soul vibrates the mental permanent unit, permanently ensconced there during and between lives, which then attracts towards its mental atoms of a similar vibratory rate that then form a mental sheath.

3. Within the mental sheath, the soul then activates on the astral plane the astral permanent unit and, in the same way, formulates the astral sheath.

4. The sheaths now hover over a fertilised human egg, pre-selected by the soul and the Lords of Karma. Progressively, the embryo and the foetus are occupied, especially during the period of quickening when the limb buds suddenly grow extensively.

5. As the child matures into the adult, the soul has ample opportunities to secure its increasing hold on the physical body. This will be affected greatly by the degree of spiritual orientation of the assumed personality.

6. The personality expresses a measure of the purpose of the soul, wears out its physical body and discards it at the end of the incarnation.

7. The consciousness after death loses the rationalising faculties of the physical plane and its etheric counterpart, but life goes on in the astro-mental body formed out of the astro-mental sheath during the incarnation.

8. The astral body has been discarded and consciousness has continued on the mental plane in the mental body.

9. The passage through the astral plane and the mental plane takes a total of about fifty years. Life in the astro-mental body is about 20-25 years. There is a further period of life in the mental body of twenty-five years.

10. The third death occurs. The last vestige of form is shed, this being the mental shell.

11. The remaining consciousness is spiritual, comprising those events conforming to Atma, Buddhi and Manas ((Will, Compassion (Love-Wisdom) and Abstract thought (Intelligence)) manifested in the life just vacated on Earth. These, as a unit of energy, enter the heaven state (Devachan) where the soul overshadows them, abstracts the spiritual components of Atma, Buddhi and Manas so that nothing eventually remains of the last personality. The soul resides entirely in the heaven world until the Will-to-Be reasserts itself and the cycle of rebirth begins again."

REINCARNATION - WHY, WHERE & HOW
WE HAVE LIVED BEFORE
By Douglas M. Baker
(some clarifications made by the author)

Reincarnation and When

Here are some factors that determine the duration before the Soul readies itself for incarnation again:

❖ *The need of humanity and the will of Hierarchy (the Masters, the spiritual guiding force of this planet) to accomplish a certain mission requiring this type of Soul.*

❖ *How much "good essence" the last incarnation provided.*

❖ *The Soul's requirements to work off karma.*

❖ *The karmic relationships with others created in the last and previous incarnations. We tend to incarnate in groups of souls to work off karma we have with each other.*

❖ *The Soul reincarnates into the time and place most suited to gain qualities it is lacking.*

❖ *Other circumstances governed by rules and laws.*

All these planes, all the different life forms and so much more, together make up in reality one mighty, wonderful, living whole.

Reincarnation is not an endless cycle. It is like an upward winding spiral, ever building upon qualities and abilities gained during previous lives. The Soul reincarnates into the time and place most suited to gain qualities it is lacking and to work out karma.

Remember a very important fact: it is the Soul that incarnates part of itself. Not the last personality, but the best it can, and is allowed to send forth to accomplish its purpose, its fixed design.

This tiny part of life's description I humbly send into the world with the hope to encourage you, my fellow truth seeker to undertake further studies and to understand yourself better. May your journey from now on have been enriched and given more meaning by this little book.

Dieter

PURPOSE:

Verily I say unto thee
Let us be like a tree
With the roots firmly planted
Into the soil of our material responsibilities
And an upward reaching trunk
That supports an ever widening, onward growing crown
Like the branches ....
Stretching out toward the light from above
And then ..... my brothers and sisters
When the time has come
Let us burst forth into a flowering glory
And our fruits ripen
And benefit those, who grow in our shadow
For that, beloved ones, is our purpose!

Through Dieter G. Gedeik
June 1976

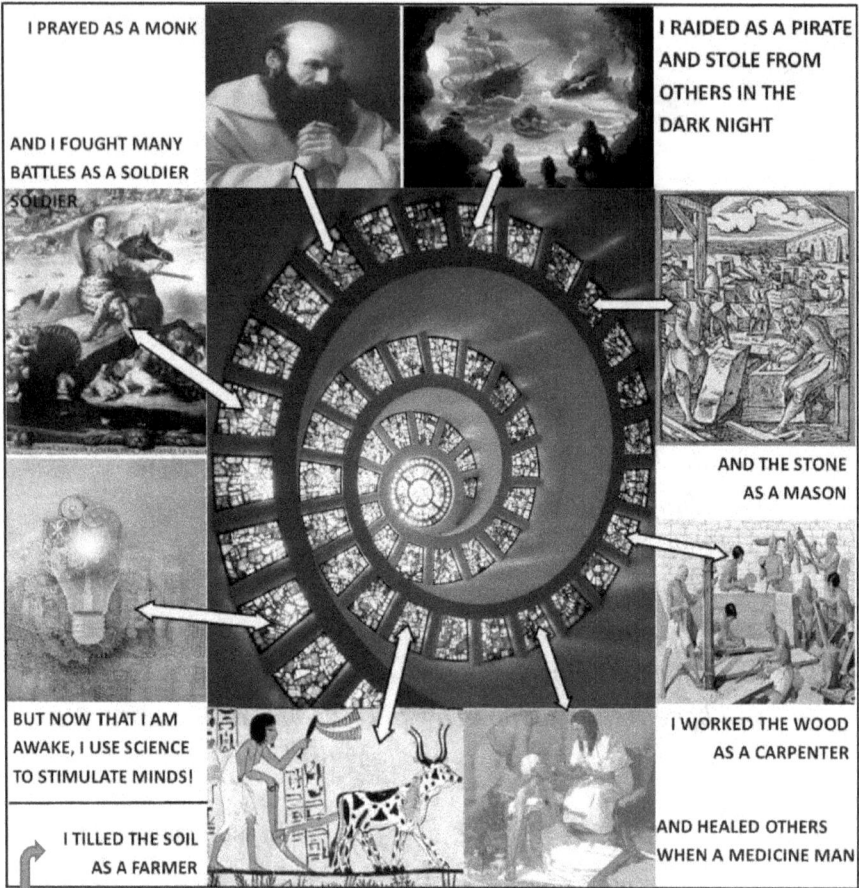

I PRAYED AS A MONK

AND I FOUGHT MANY BATTLES AS A SOLDIER

I RAIDED AS A PIRATE AND STOLE FROM OTHERS IN THE DARK NIGHT

AND THE STONE AS A MASON

BUT NOW THAT I AM AWAKE, I USE SCIENCE TO STIMULATE MINDS!

I WORKED THE WOOD AS A CARPENTER

I TILLED THE SOIL AS A FARMER

AND HEALED OTHERS WHEN A MEDICINE MAN

START HERE

And May You Also One Day Remember….

I know I am deathless,
I know this orbit of mine cannot be swept by a carpenter's compass...
And whether I come to my own to-day or in ten thousand or ten million years,
I can cheerfully take it now, or with equal cheerfulness I can wait…

Song of Myself
Walt Whitman

From the unreal lead me to the Real
From darkness lead me to Light
From death lead me to Immortality.

REFERENCES USED

A list of some of the works quoted from: (Part # 6061)

The Process of Dying and our Journey Beyond
What really happens when we shed our physical body!

Death: The Great Adventure. A compilation by two students, from the writings of Alice A. Bailey and the Tibetan Master, Djwhal Khul. ISBN 0-85330-138-7, The Lucis Publishing Co.

The Soul, the Quality of Life. A compilation by a student, from the writings of Alice A. Bailey and the Tibetan Master, Djwhal Khul. No ISBN. The Lucis Publishing Co.

Ponder on this. A compilation by a student, from the writings of Alice A. Bailey and the Tibetan Master, Djwhal Khul. ISBN 0-85330-131-X, The Lucis Publishing Co.

The Nature of The Soul. Lucille Cedercrans, Wisdom Impressions, ISBN 1-883493-02-1 http://www.wisdomimpressions.com/

Occult Glossary. By G. de Purucker, PDF eBook ISBN 978-1-55700-214-3, THEOSOPHICAL UNIVERSITY PRESS. Out of print, try used: ISBN 1-55700-050-6 (cloth: alk. paper) ISBN 1-55700-051-4 (paper: alk. paper) or as eBook.

The Hidden Side of Things. C. W. Leadbeater, ISBN0-8356-7007-4, The Theosophical Publishing House.

The Astral Plane. C. W. Leadbeater, ISBN 0-8356-7093-7, The Theosophical Publishing House. http://www.questbooks.net/authors.cfm?letter=l

The Life after Death. C. W. Leadbeater, ISBN 0-8356-7148-8, The Theosophical Publishing House.

The Devachanic Plane. C. W. Leadbeater, ISBN 0-8356-7075-9, The Theosophical Publishing House.

The Monad. C. W. Leadbeater, ISBN 0-8356-0102-1, The Theosophical Publishing House.

Death – and After. Annie Besant, ISBN 0-8356-7039-2
The Theosophical Publishing House

A Study in Consciousness. Annie Besant, The Theosophical
Publishing House, ISBN 0-8356-7287-5
http://www.questbooks.net/authors.cfm?letter=b

The Nature of Memory. Annie Besant & H. P. Blavatsky, The
Theosophical Publishing House, ISBN 81-7059-023-X

Man, Visible and Invisible. C. W. Leadbeater, The Theosophical
Publishing House, ISBN 0-8536-0311-3,
http://www.questbooks.net/authors.cfm?letter=l

Man: Whence, How and Whither. C. W. Leadbeater & A. Besant,
The Theosophical Publishing House, ISBN 0-8356-7173-9

The Secret Doctrine. H. P. Blavatsky:
http://www.questbooks.net/authors.cfm?letter=b
Vol. I. - Cosmogenesis, Theosophical University Press
Vol. II. - Anthropogenesis, Theosophical University Press

Esoteric Healing. Alice A. Bailey, Lucis Publishing Company,
ISBN 978-0-853-30121-9
https://www.lucistrust.org/store/item/esoteric_healing

The Light of the Soul, The Yoga Sutras of Patanjali. Alice A.
Bailey, Lucis Publishing Company, ISBN 0-85330-112-3
https://www.lucistrust.org/store/category/alice_bailey_books_p

Glamour, a World Problem, Alice A. Bailey, Lucis Publishing
Company,http://www.lucistrust.org/en/publications_store/alice_bailey_bo
oks_p

The Jewel in the Lotus, Dr. Douglas M. Baker, ISBN 0-906006-71-
6, buy used or as the eBook from Amazon or iTunes Store. ISBN
9781625690234, Baker eBooks Publishing.

Life After Death, Dr. Douglas M. Baker, ISBN 0-906006-58-9
(printed ver.), ISBN 9781255690142 (eBook ver.) Baker eBooks
Publishing. Amazon or iTunes Store.

The Wheel of Rebirth, Dr. Douglas M. Baker, ISBN 0-906006-16-3, (printed ver.), ISBN 9781625690340, (eBook ver.) Baker eBooks Publishing. Amazon or iTunes Store.

Reincarnation – Why, Where and How we have Lived Before, Dr. Douglas M. Baker, ISBN 0-906006-57-0, (printed ver.), ISBN 9781625690173, (eBook ver.) Baker eBooks Publishing.

The Rainbow Bridge, First and Second Phases, Link with the Soul & Purification, by Two Disciples. Rainbow Bridge Productions, ISBN 0-87613-078-3 (Make sure you get the Phase I & Phase II addition in one book!) Out of print, buy used.

"What Dreams May Come" A movie with Robin Williams, Cuba Gooding, Jr. and Annabella Sciorra. **Good DVD** to get for its "reasonable" depiction of the Astral Plane. Suicide and when to reincarnate is not accurately depicted. **A very inspiring and beautiful film!** ISBN 0-7832-7754-7, You can see it on Netflix and other providers.

http://www.abebooks.com/ I found this to be the best source for new, used, and out-of-print books.

All Besant, Leadbeater, Blavatsky and other books, search availability at **www.theosophicalsearch.org**

All 24 Alice A. Bailey books are available on line: http://www.lucistrust.org/en/publications_store/books_on_line

Dieter G. Gedeik, https//:www.douglasbaker.org

INDEX

dying of cancer, 26

E

earth-bound, 17,24, 30, 31, 46, 59, 64
eidolon, 34
electric shock, 23
Elemental, 20, 23, 28, 31, 32, 34, 42, 43,
    44, 45, 56, 57, 60, 69, 78, 83, 84
elemental forces, 34
Elimination, 15 21, 26, 32, 49, 54, 57,
    76, 81, 82, 84
emotional suffering, 26
energy follows thought, 5
eternity, 71
etheric body, 16, 19, 21, 23, 27, 32, 33,
    48, 61
evil act, 31
evolved animals, 43
excessive alcohol, 48
expansion of consciousness, 73

F

false teachings, 7, 10, 13
family members, 27, 53
fear of dying, 57
Fixed Design, 1, 25, 90
forces of darkness, 45
fuller life, 56

G

GENETICS, 8
Giving blood, 33
group souls, 83

H

Hades, 42
heart-attacks, 60
heaven, 13, 25, 38, 69, 71, 80, 88, 89
Heaven-world, 71
Hell, 35, 37, 38, 39, 41
Higher Consciousness, 9
HIGHER SELF, xiii, 9, 11
homosexual karma, 28
horrific pictures, 53

human ego, 20
human evolution, 5
human kingdom, 4, 43, 58, 87
human shadows, 34

I

idols, 44, 78
illusion, 10, 42, 71, 77, 78, 80
immortality, 12, 34, 93
incarnation, 7, 9, 13, 15, 17, 21, 27, 28,
    35, 43, 55, 69, 71, 77, 78, 81, 82, 83,
    84, 85, 87, 88, 89,90
incense, 18
individualization, 83
Integration, 15, 26, 49, 68, 76, 77, 82,
    84, 85
intellectuals, 57
Internet, 26

J

Jannah, 71

K

karmic consequences, 26, 35, 59, 63, 66
karmic law, 25, 40
keeping of the book, 40

L

labor and birth, 27
life-force, 58
life-thread, 19
Lipika Lords of Karma, 40
Logos, 42, 85
lost soul, 17, 39, 40
love and Light, 61

M

macrocosm, 4
Manas, 80, 81, 89
mantras, 18
Master's ashram, 31, 69, 81
materialistic pursuit, 30
memories, 21, 60, 79